Copyright © 2023, PLEASURE BOAT STUDIO
All Rights Reserved.

ISBN 978-1-7370520-0-5
Library of Congress Control Number 2023906335

Book design & concept by Lauren Grosskopf

Pleasure Boat Studio books are available through the following:
Ingram Worldwide Distribution, Baker & Taylor, Amazon.com, bn.com &
PLEASURE BOAT STUDIO: A NONPROFIT LITERARY PRESS
PLEASUREBOATSTUDIO.COM
Seattle, Washington

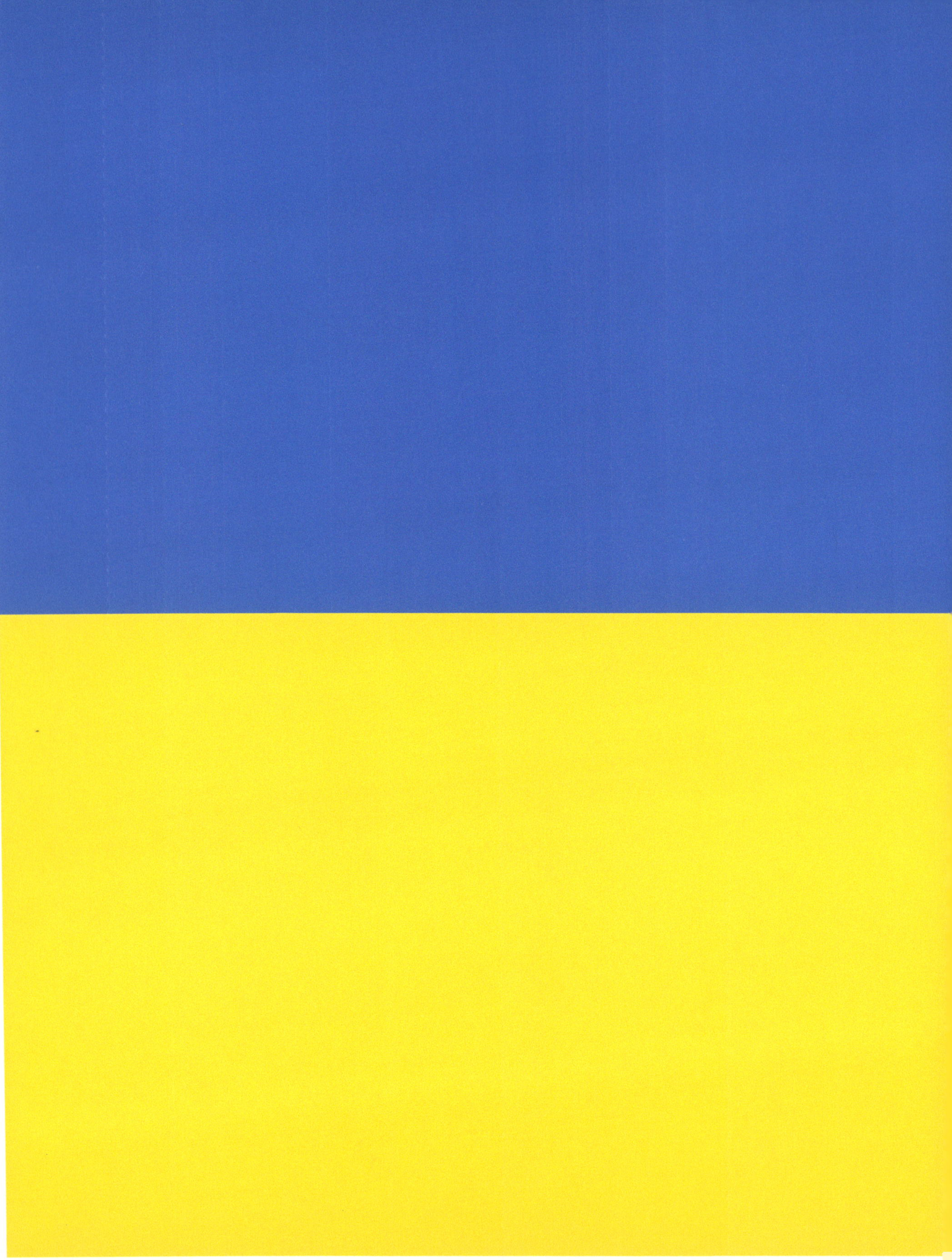

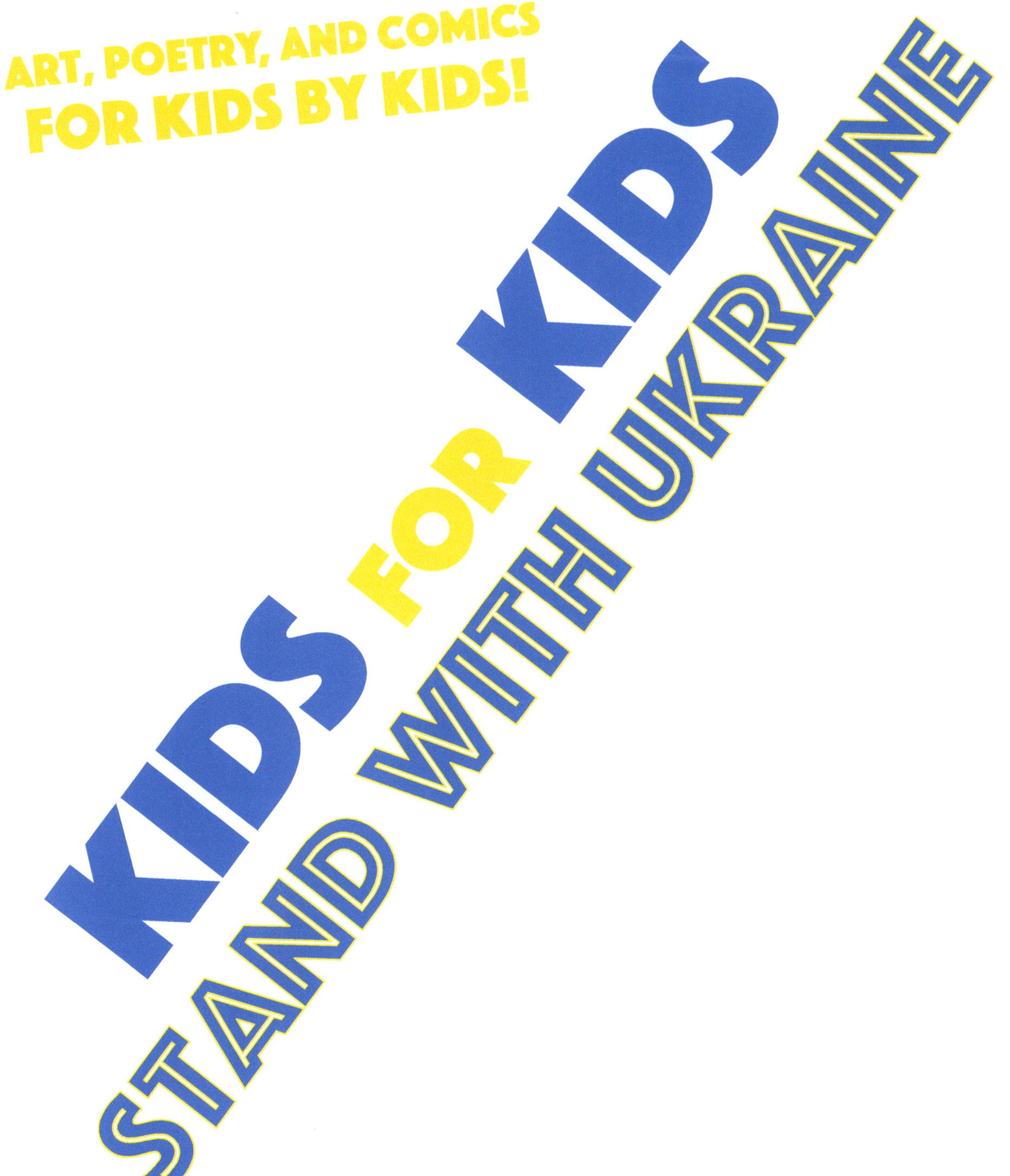

ART, POETRY, AND COMICS FOR KIDS BY KIDS!

KIDS FOR KIDS

STAND WITH UKRAINE

PLEASURE BOAT STUDIO: A NONPROFIT LITERARY PRESS

Привіт, з любов'ю зі Сполучених Штатів!
Сподіваємось, це принесе вам радість.

(Pryvit, z lyubov'yu zi Spoluchenykh Shtativ!
Spodivayemos', tse prynese vam radist'.)

Hello, with love from the United States!
We hope this will bring you joy.

TABLE OF CONTENTS

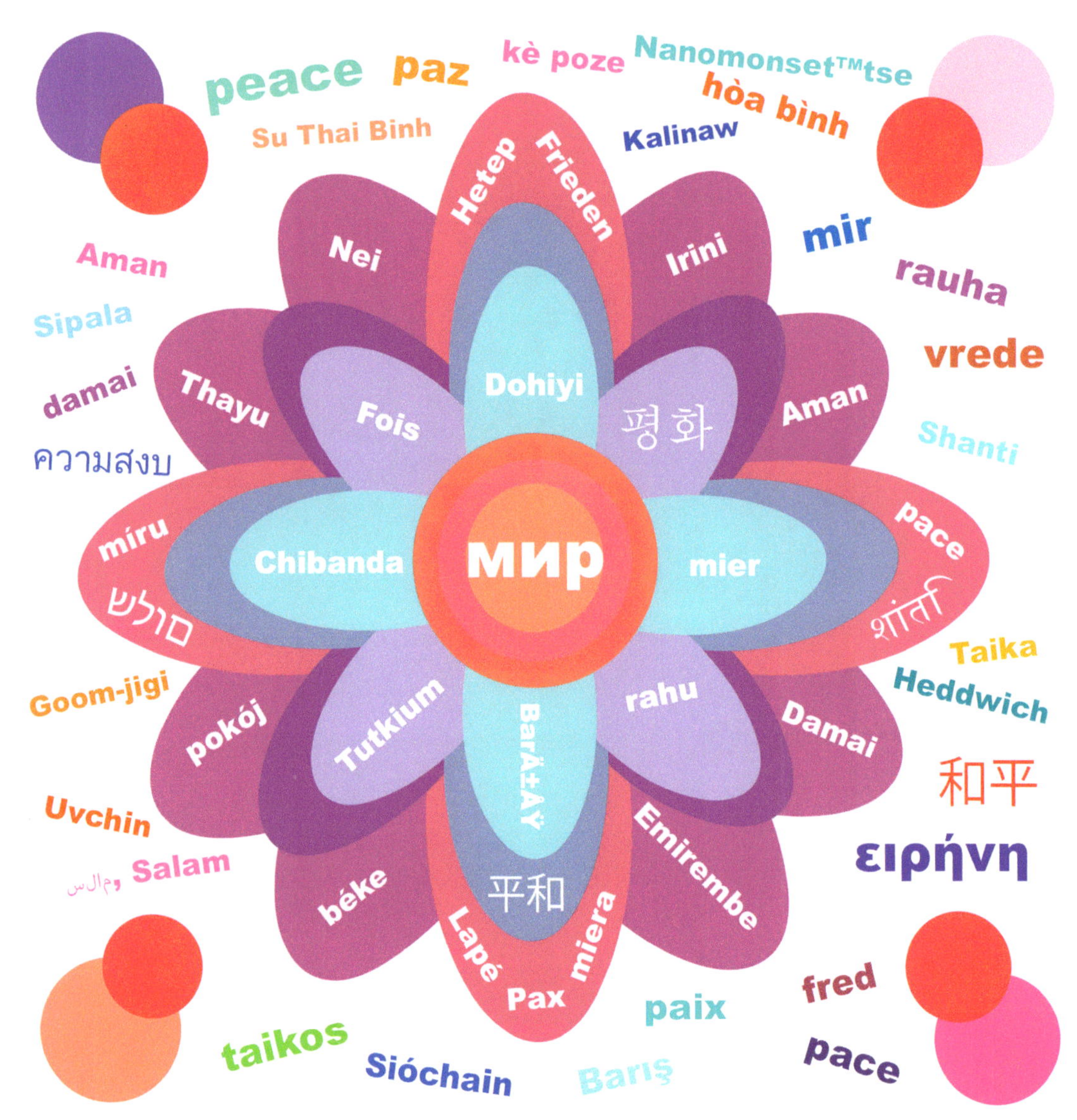

peace
paz
kè poze
Nanomonset™tse
hòa bình
Su Thai Binh
Kalinaw
mir
rauha
Aman
Nei
Hetep
Frieden
Irini
vrede
Sipala
Dohiyi
평화
Aman
Shanti
damai
Thayu
Fois
ความสงบ
míru
Chibanda
МИР
mier
pace
שלום
शांति
Goom-jigi
Tutkium
BarĂ±AЎ
rahu
Taika
Heddwich
pokój
Damai
和平
Uvchin
béke
平和
Emirembe
εɩρήνη
سلام, Salam
Lapé
Pax
miera
paix
fred
taikos
Sióchain
Barış
pace

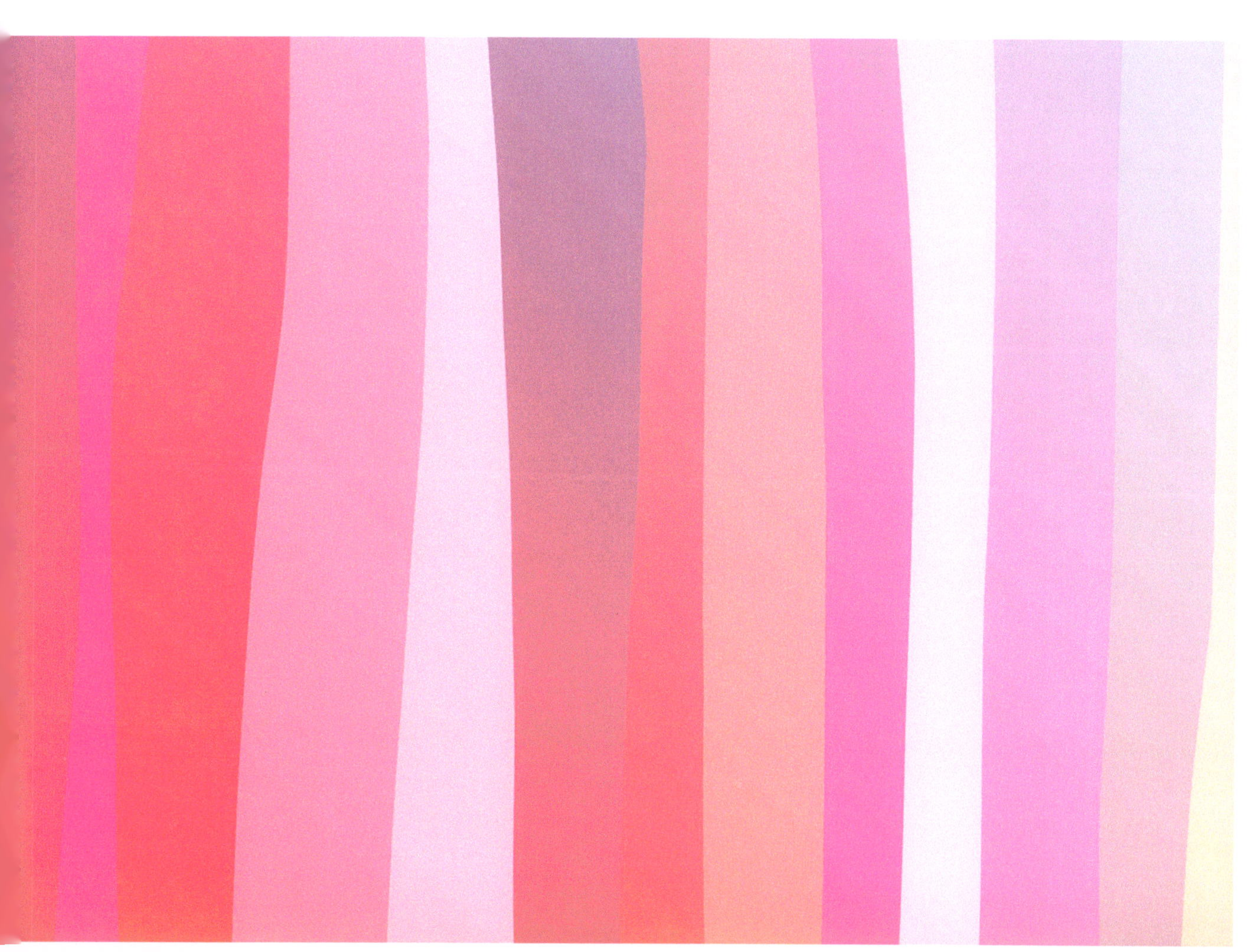

KIDS FOR KIDS
STAND WITH UKRAINE

NINA KUZMYCZ

Age 11, West Seattle, WA

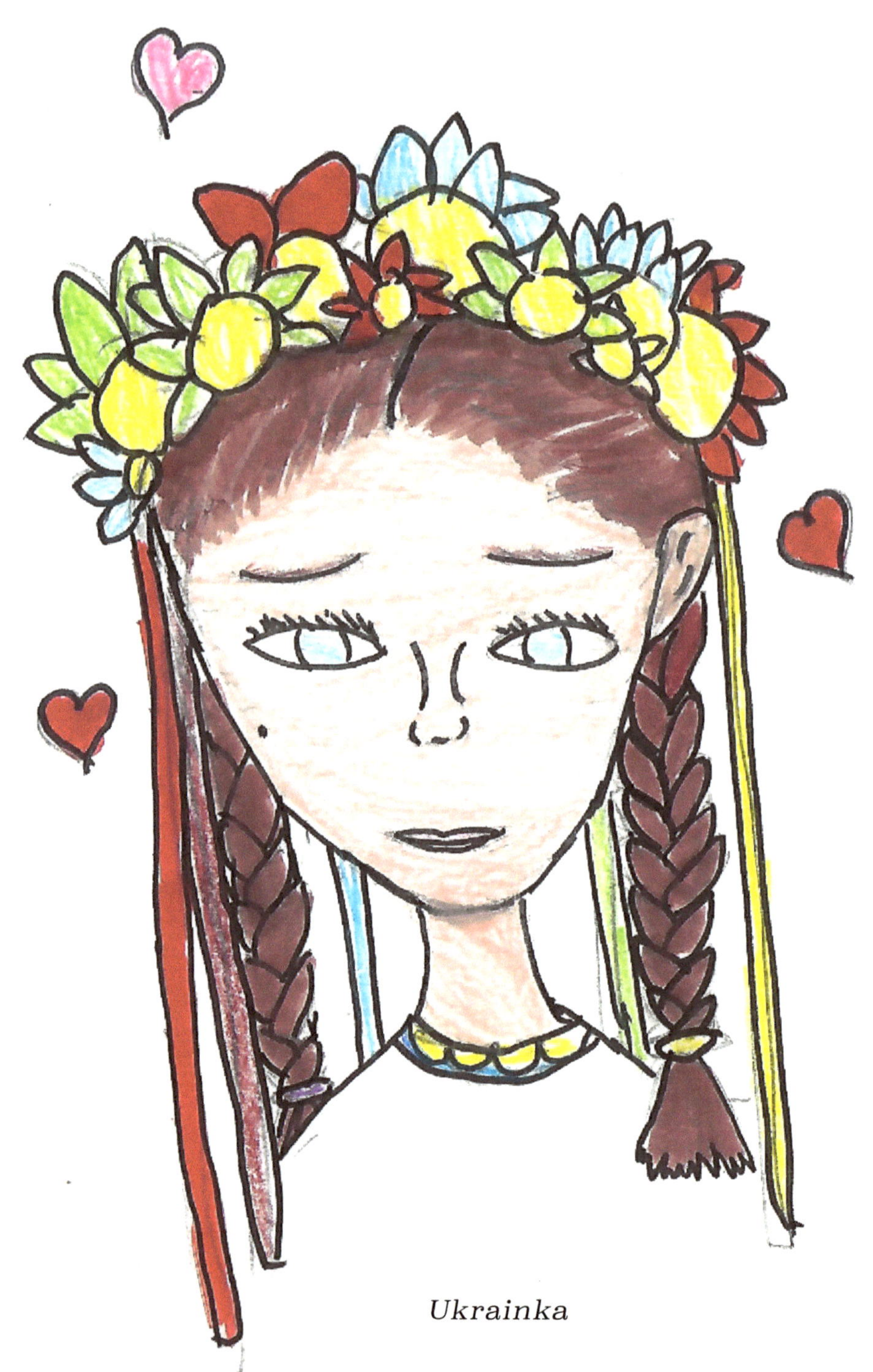

Ukrainka

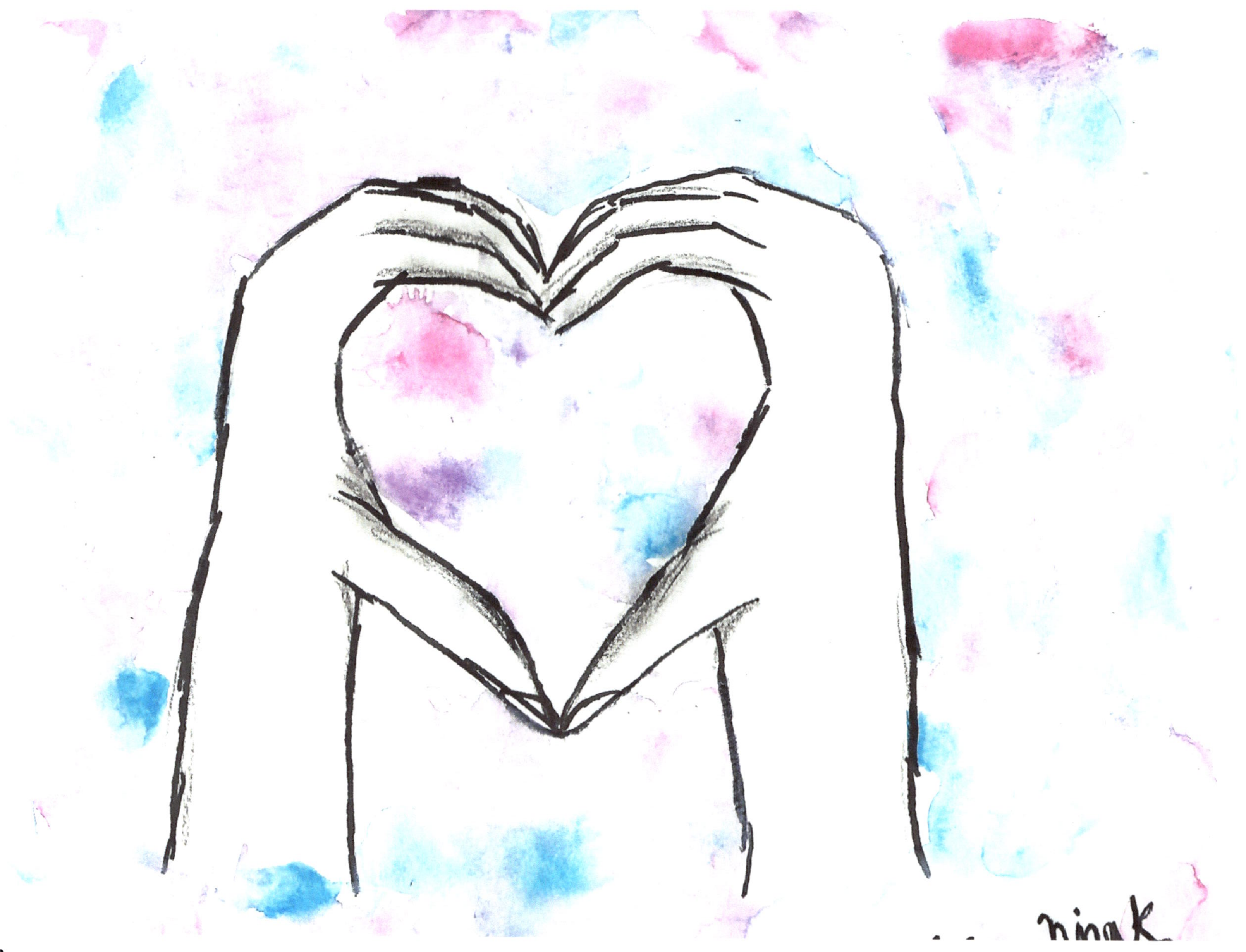

nina k

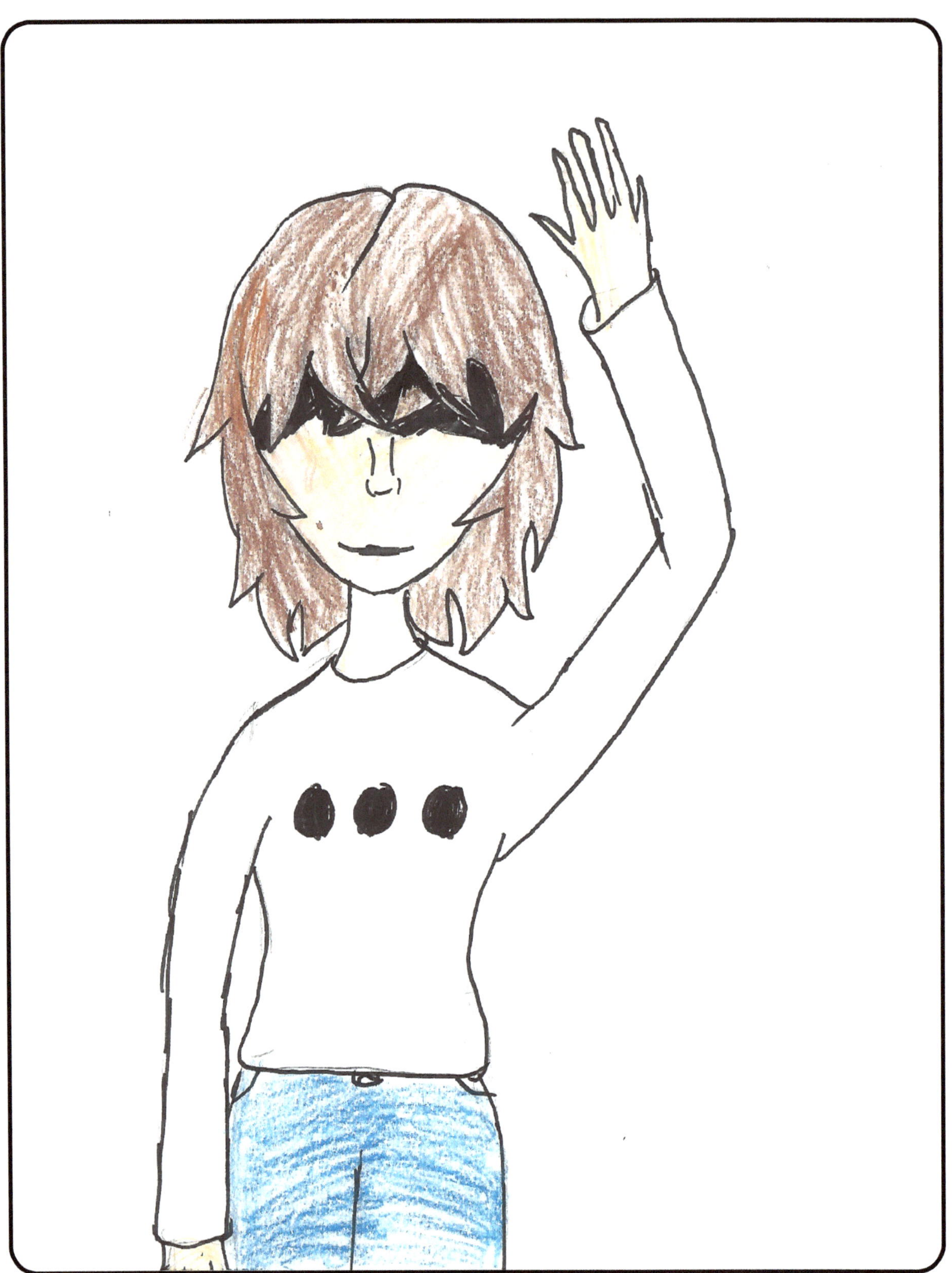

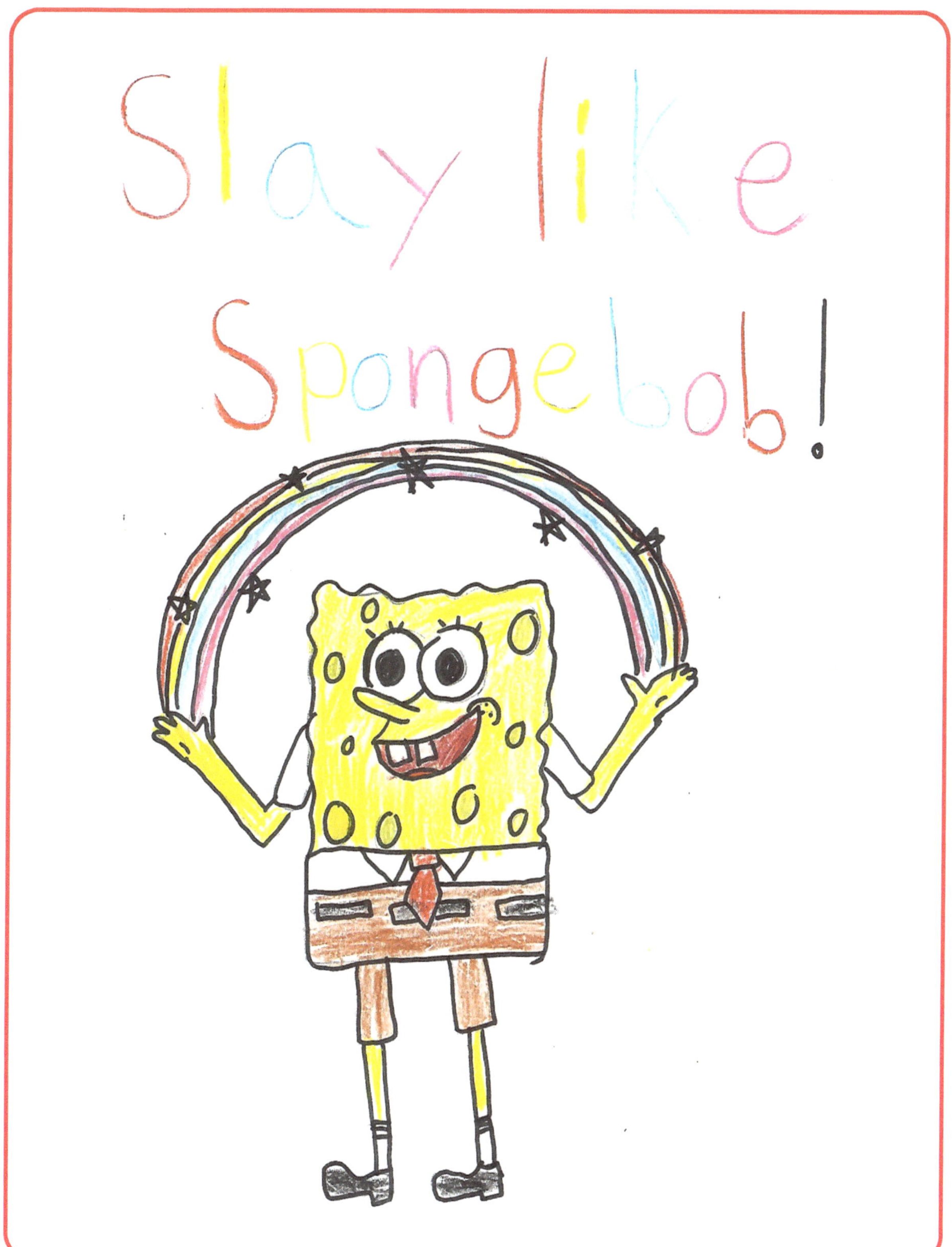

Slay like
SpongeBob!

MAUDE WELKER

Age 12, West Seattle, WA

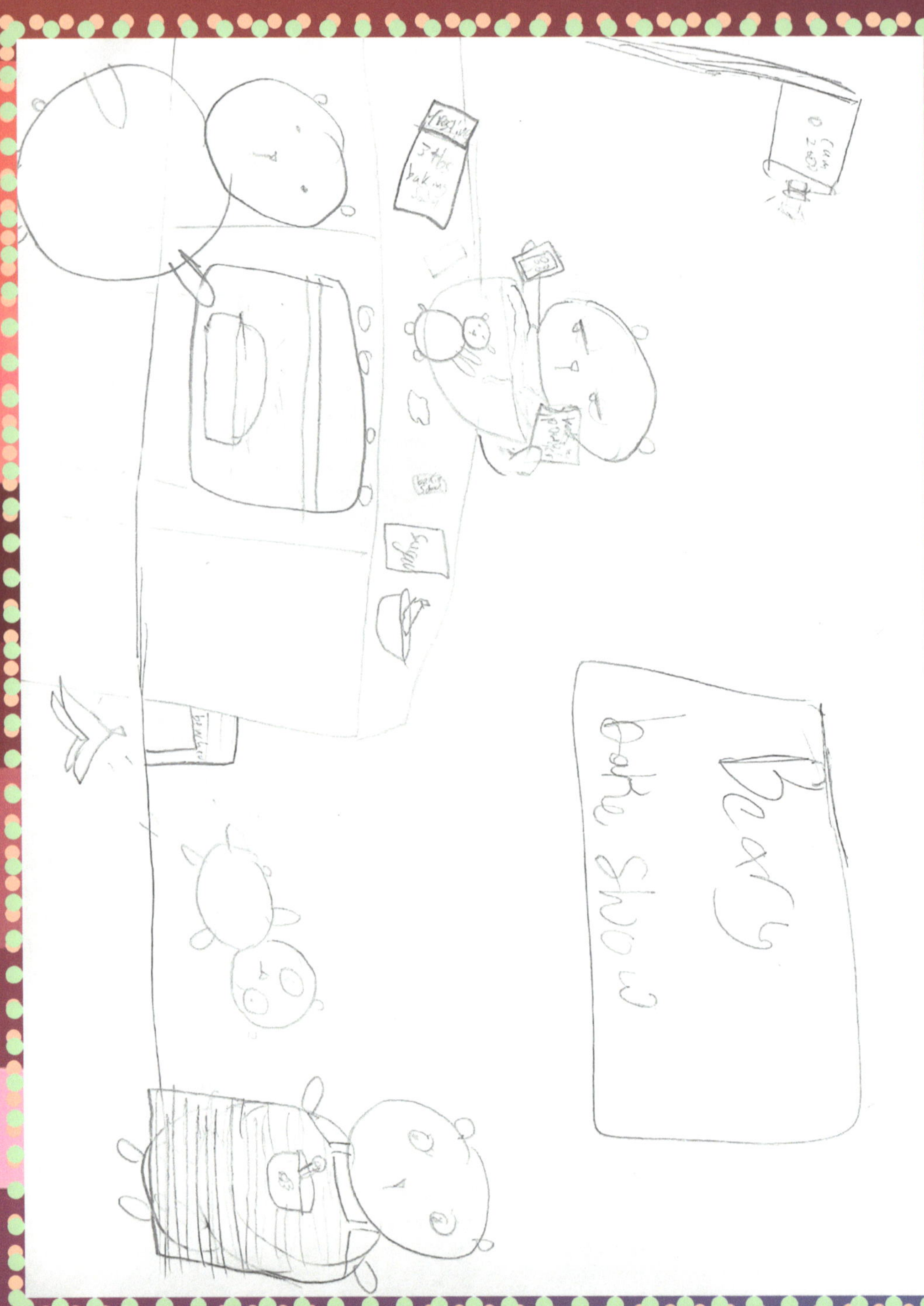

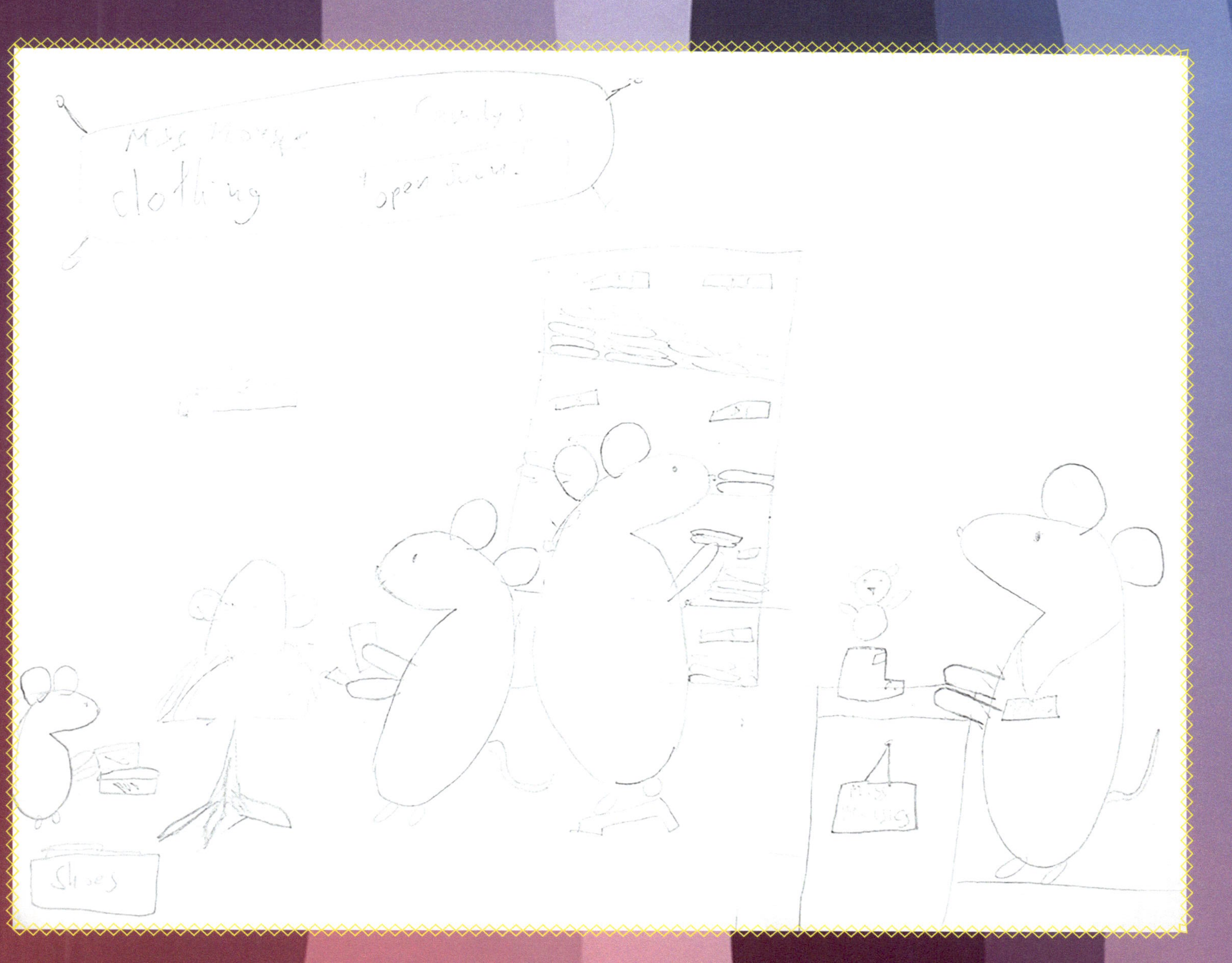

Mrs Mouse
clothing
open store.
Shoes

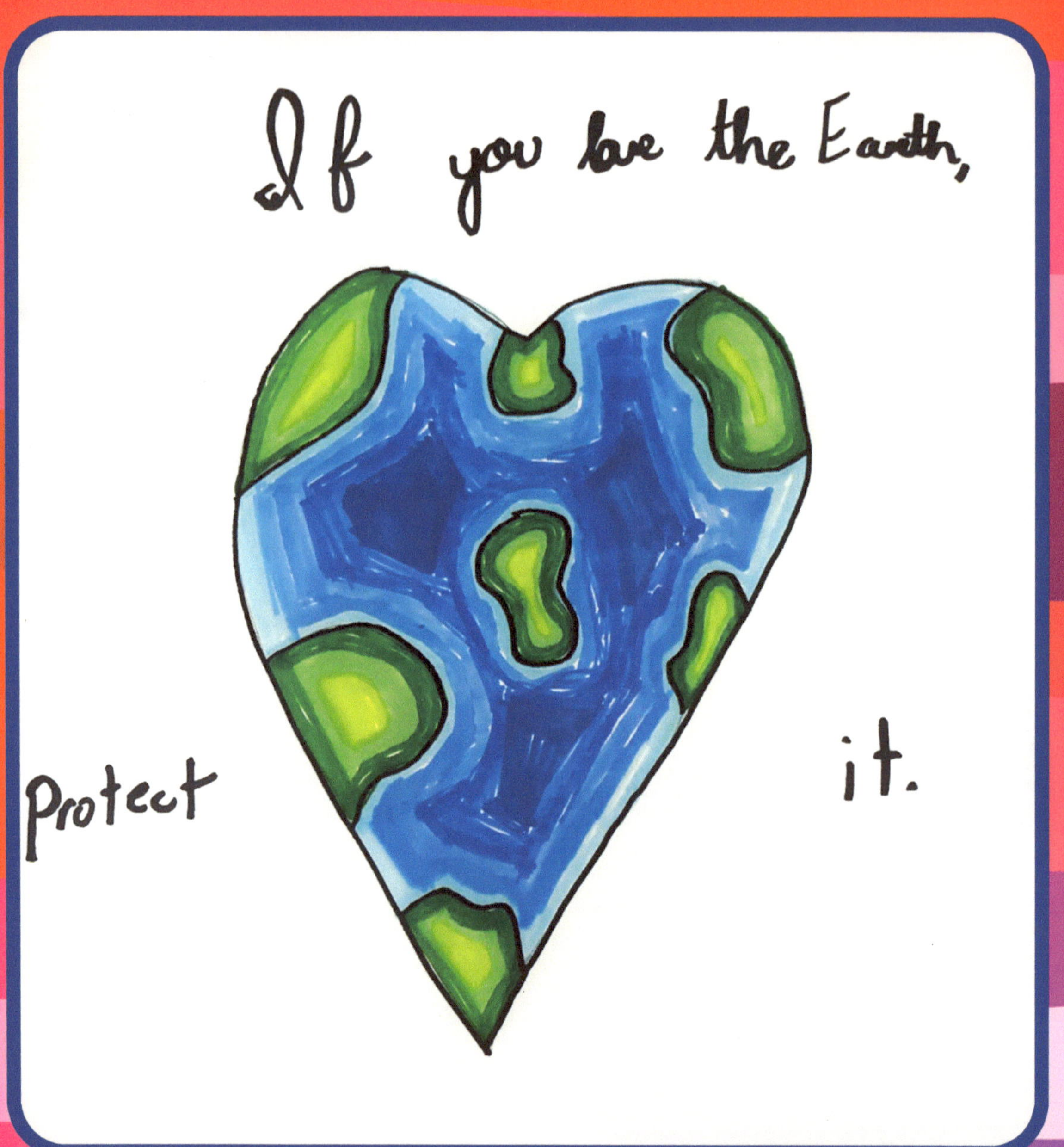
If you love the Earth,
protect it.

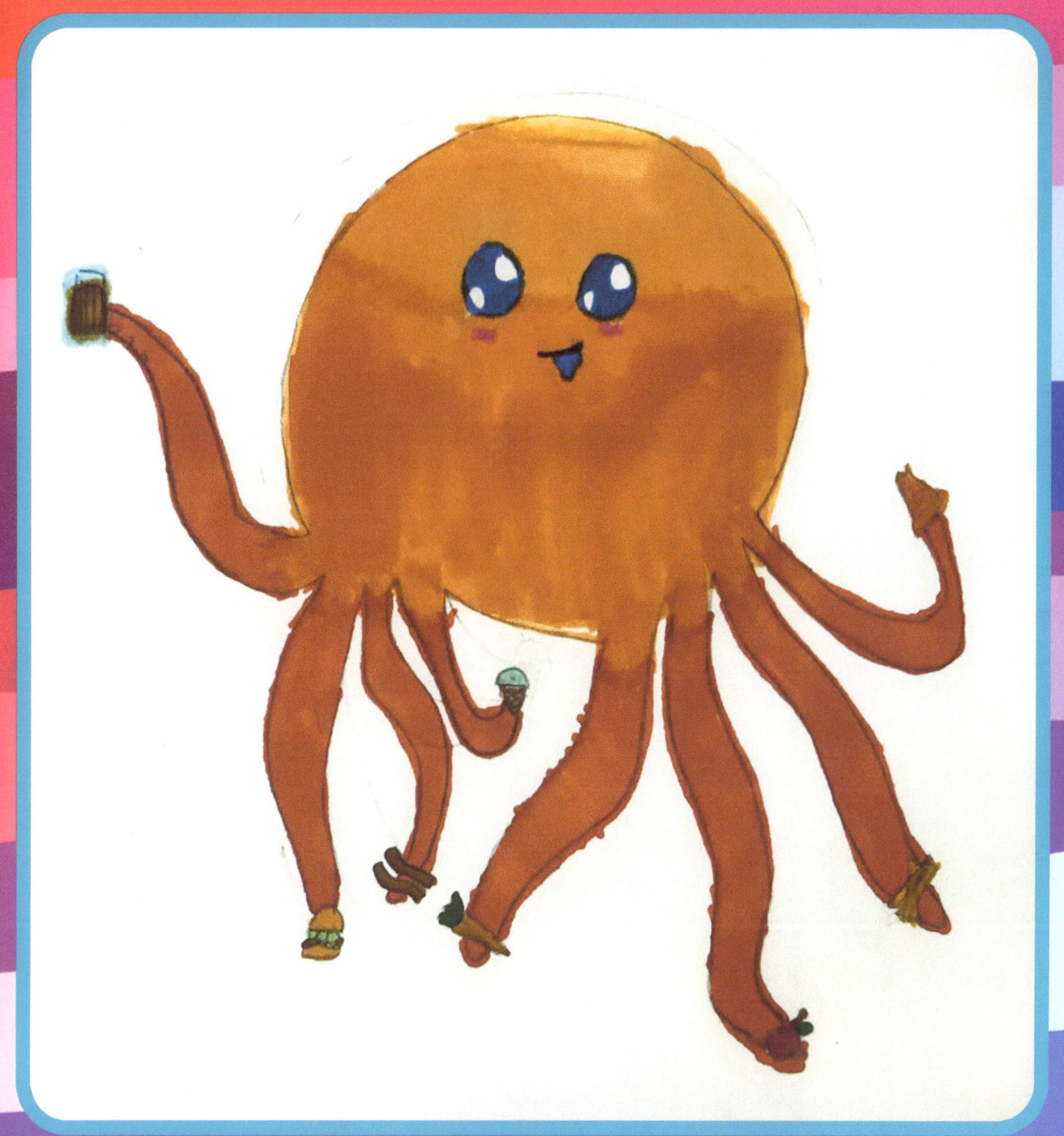

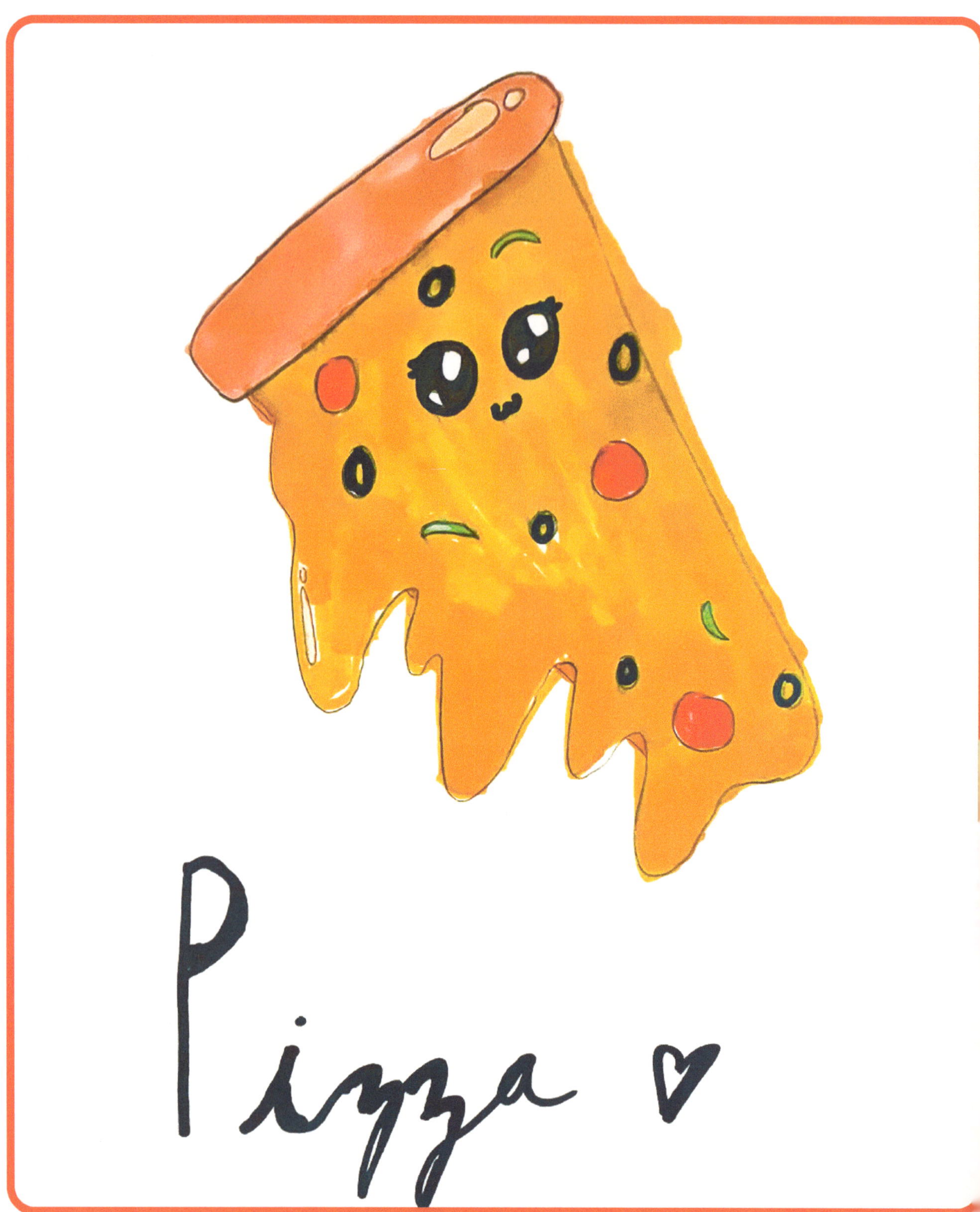

Pizza ♡

The

Aries
March 21 - April 20
Taurus
April 21 - May 20
Gemini
May 21 - June 20
Cancer
June 21 - July 22
Leo
July 23 - August 22
Virgo
August 23 - September 22
Libra
September 23 - October 22
Scorpio
october 23 - Nov 20
Sagittarius
Nov. 21 - Dec 20
Capricorn
Dec. 21 - Jan. 20
Aquarius
Jan. 21 - Feb 18
Pisces
Feb 19 - Mar. 20

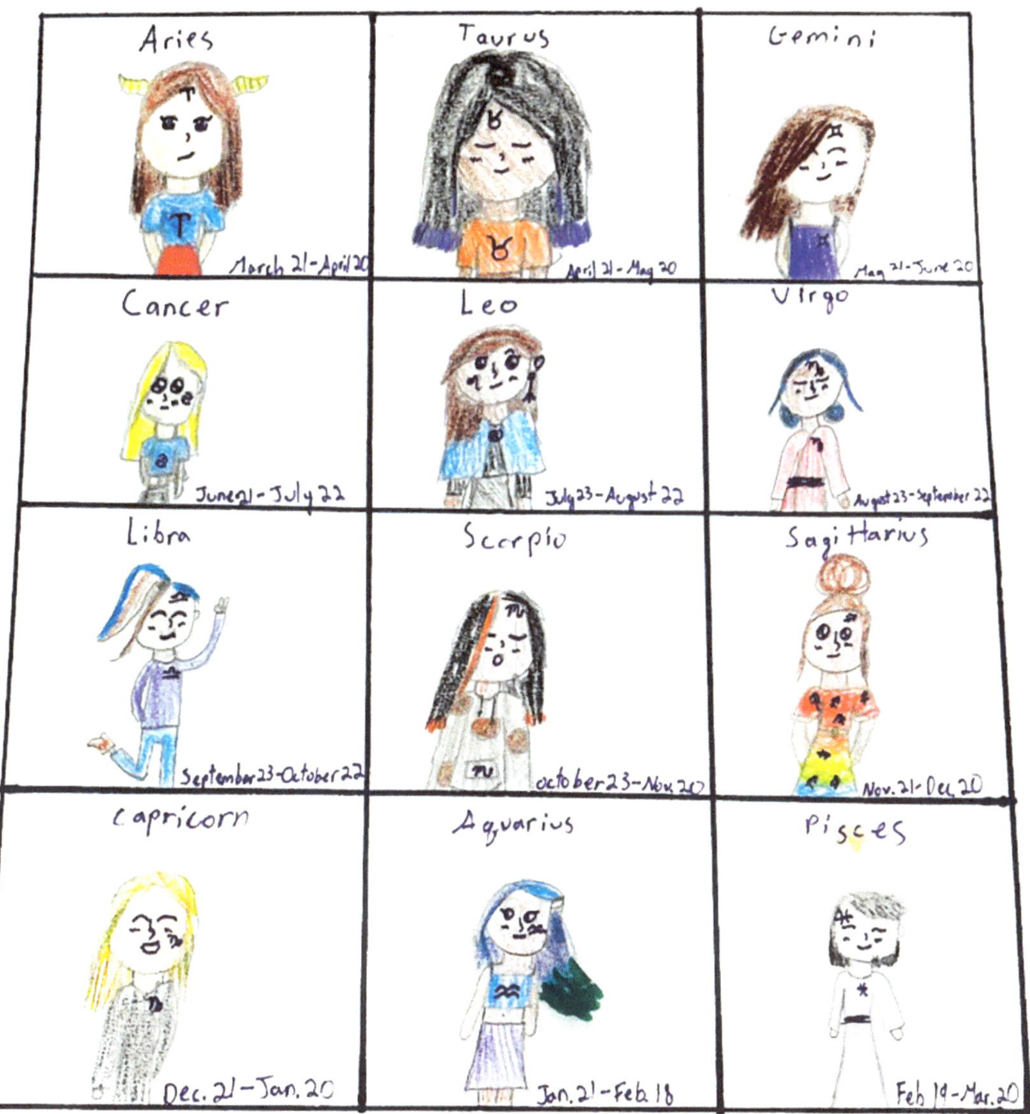

Zodiacs

THEO WILSON

Age 7, West Seattle, WA

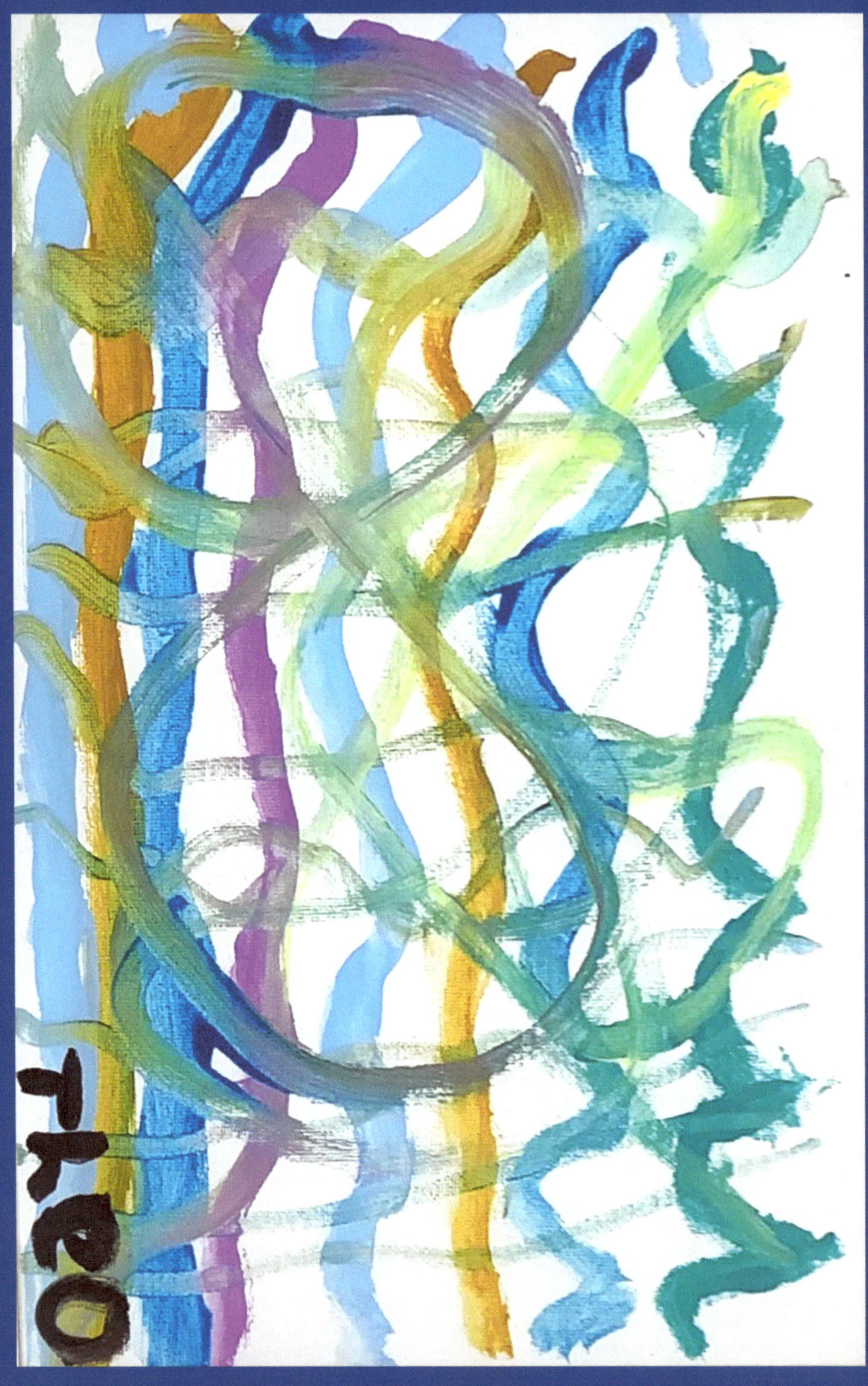

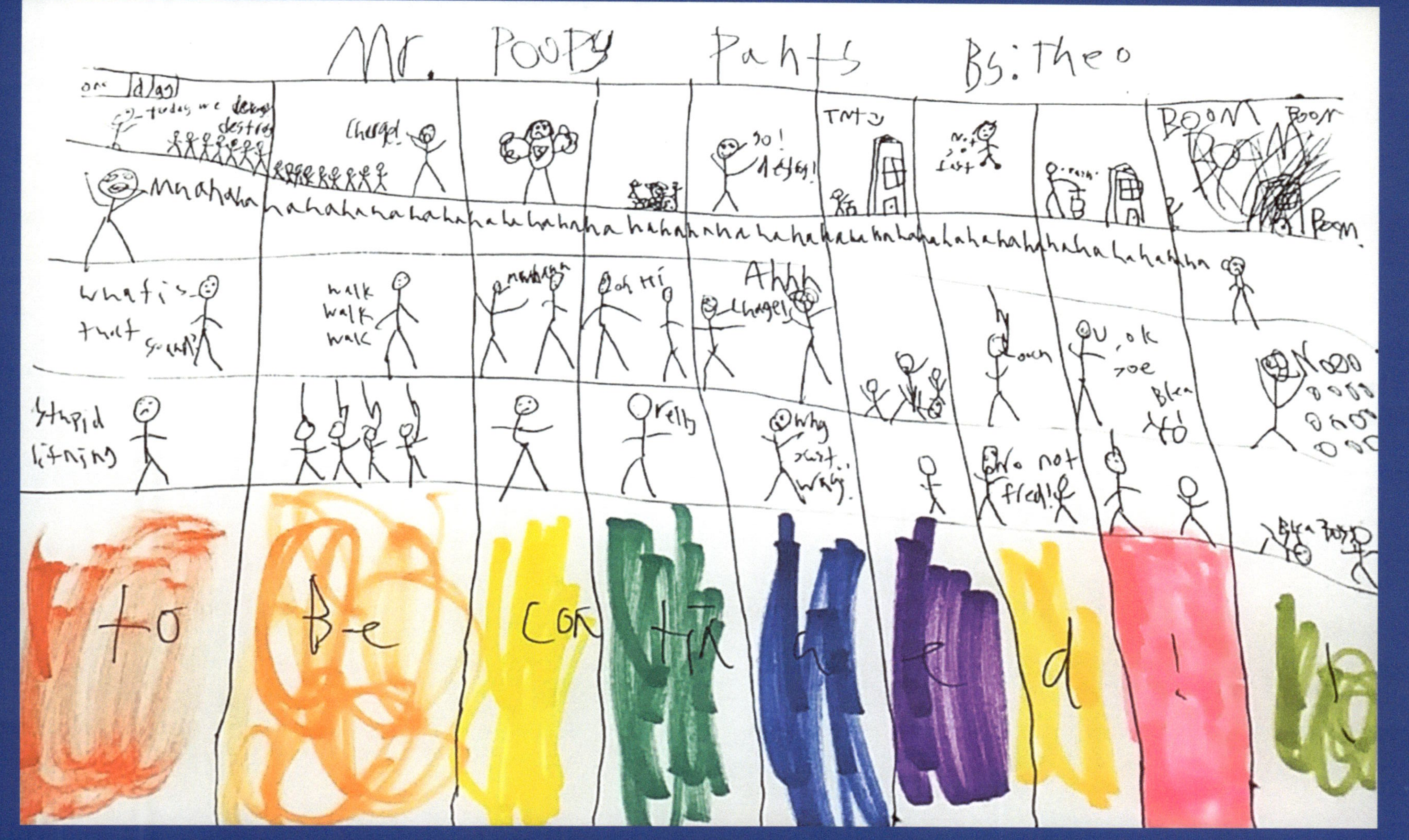

Mr. Poopy Pants   Bs: Theo
one day
today we destroy
Mhahaha hahahahahahahahahahahahahahahahahahahahaha
Charge!
so!
TNT
Not list
BOOM BOOM Boom
Boom
what is that sound?
walk walk walk
oh hi
Ahh charge!
ouch
Uh ok roe
Blea to
stupid litning
orelb
why xert.. why.
Uro not fredll
No
Bye-bye
to Be contined!

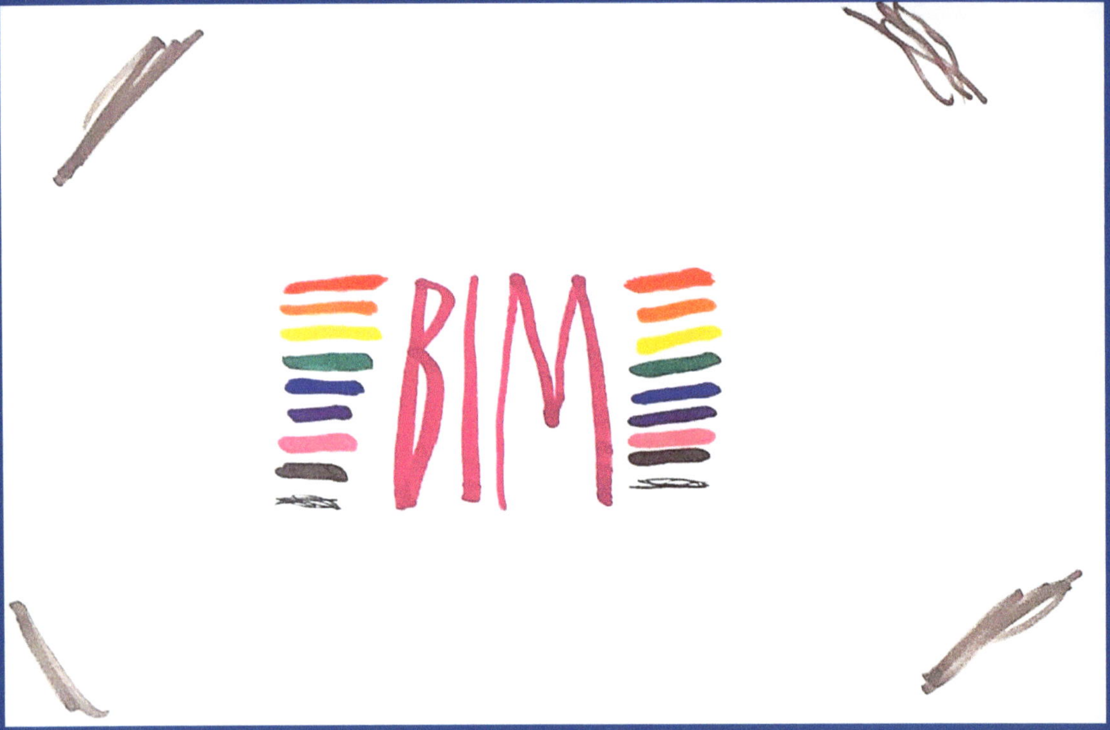

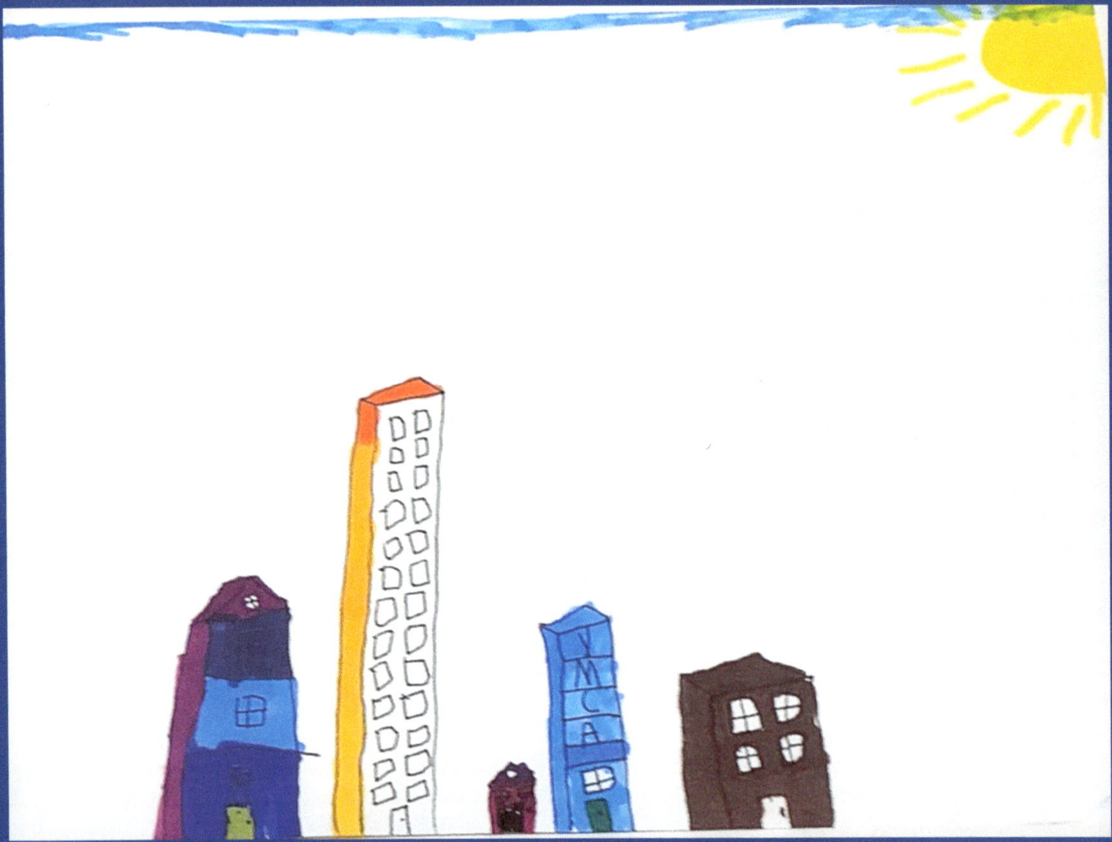

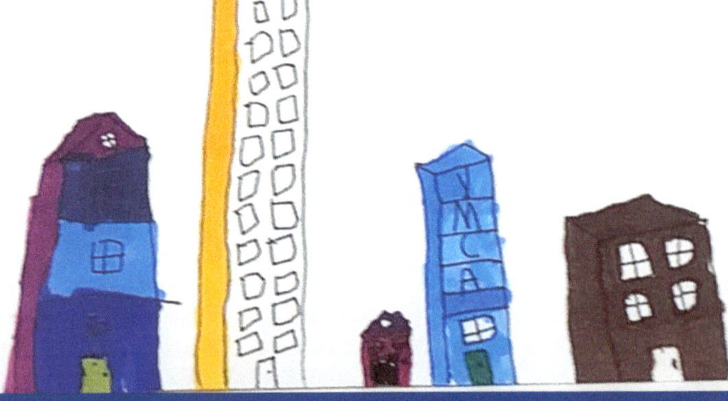

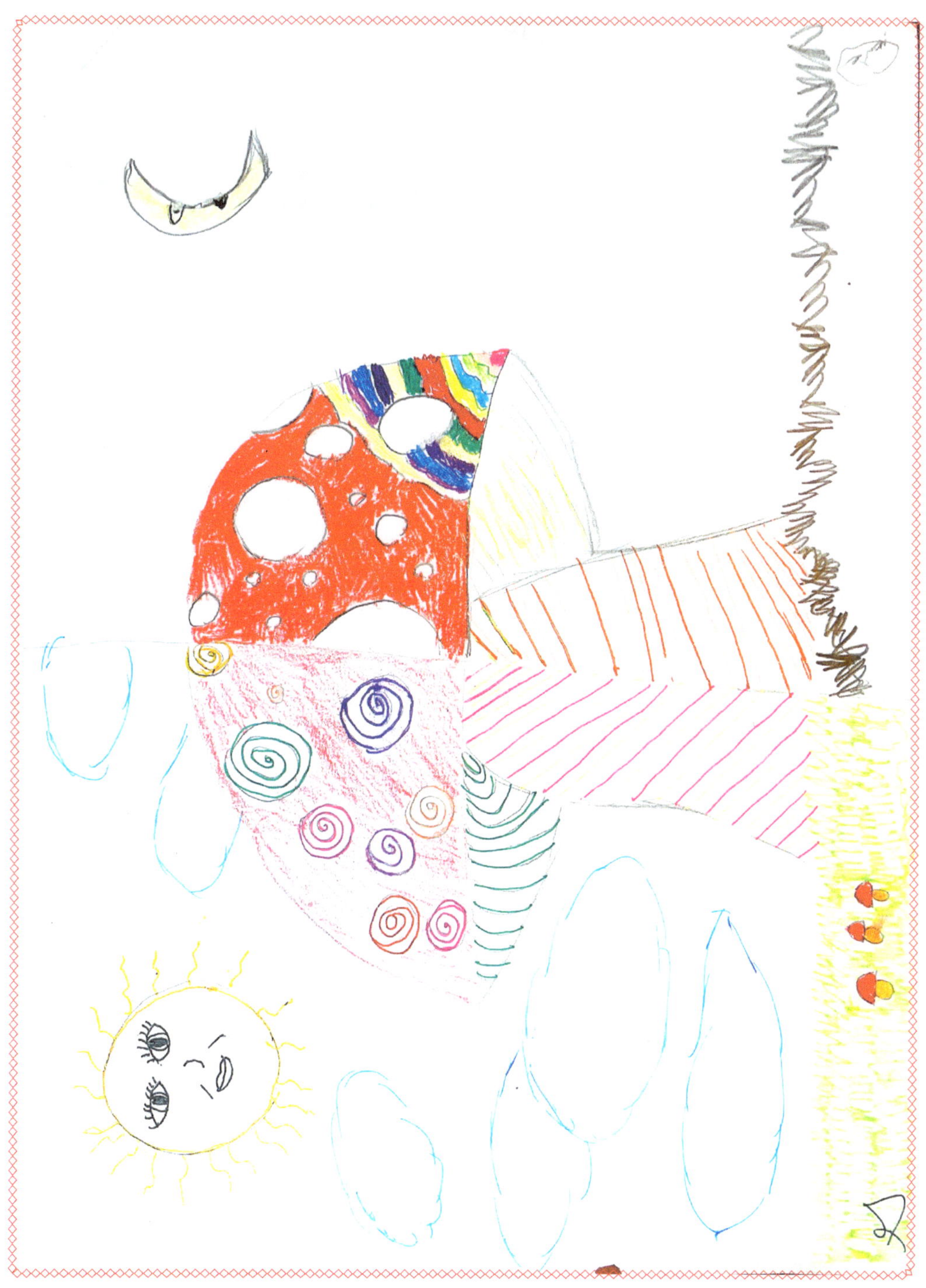

GABBY REID & MAUDE WELKER

Age 12, West Seattle, WA

JUSTINE QUAN

Age: 10, Seattle, WA

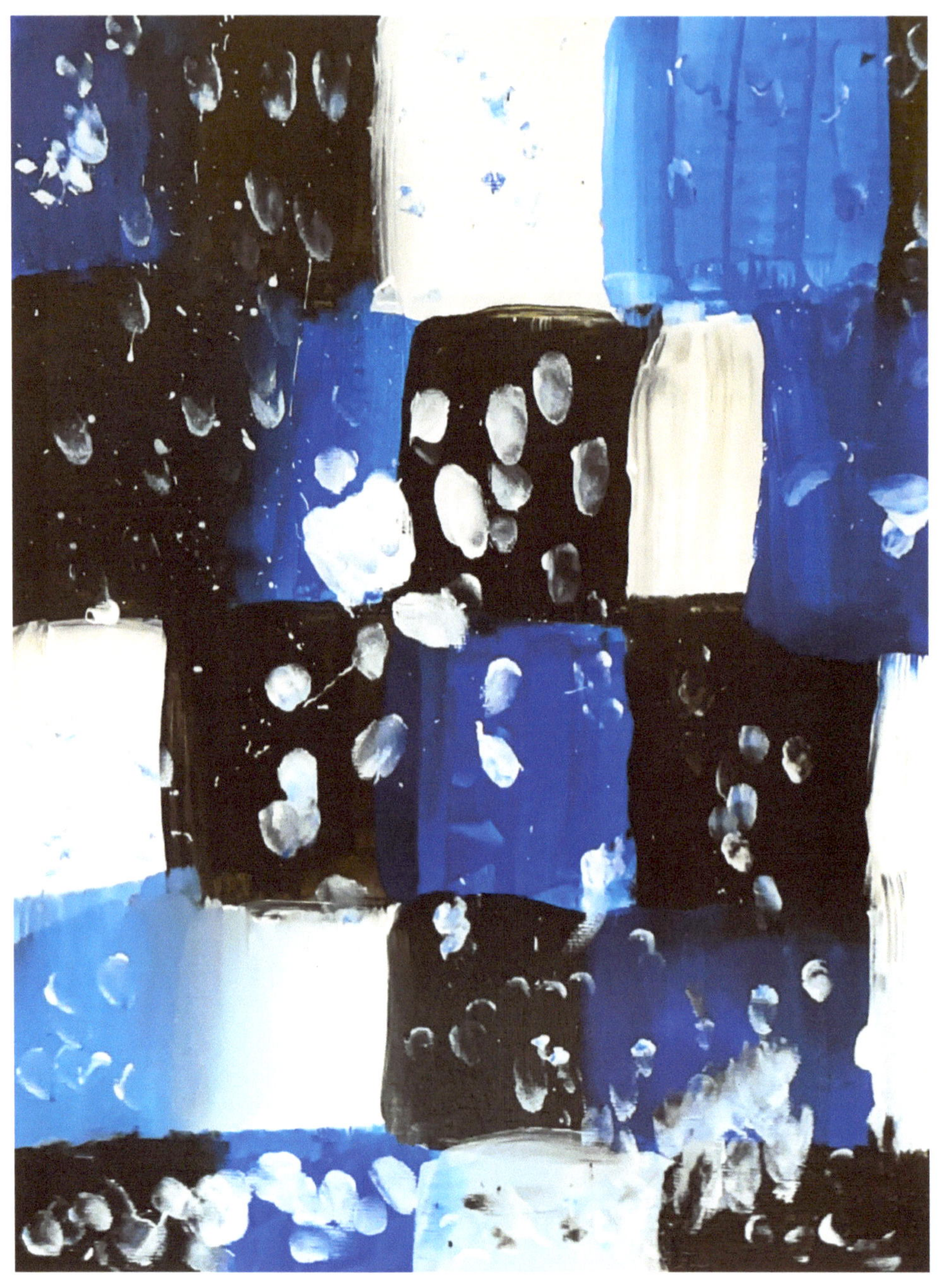

*Inspired by a reflection in the mirror that looked
like a moving wall. Turn art horizontal.*

KLARA TUININGA

Age 15, North Bend, WA

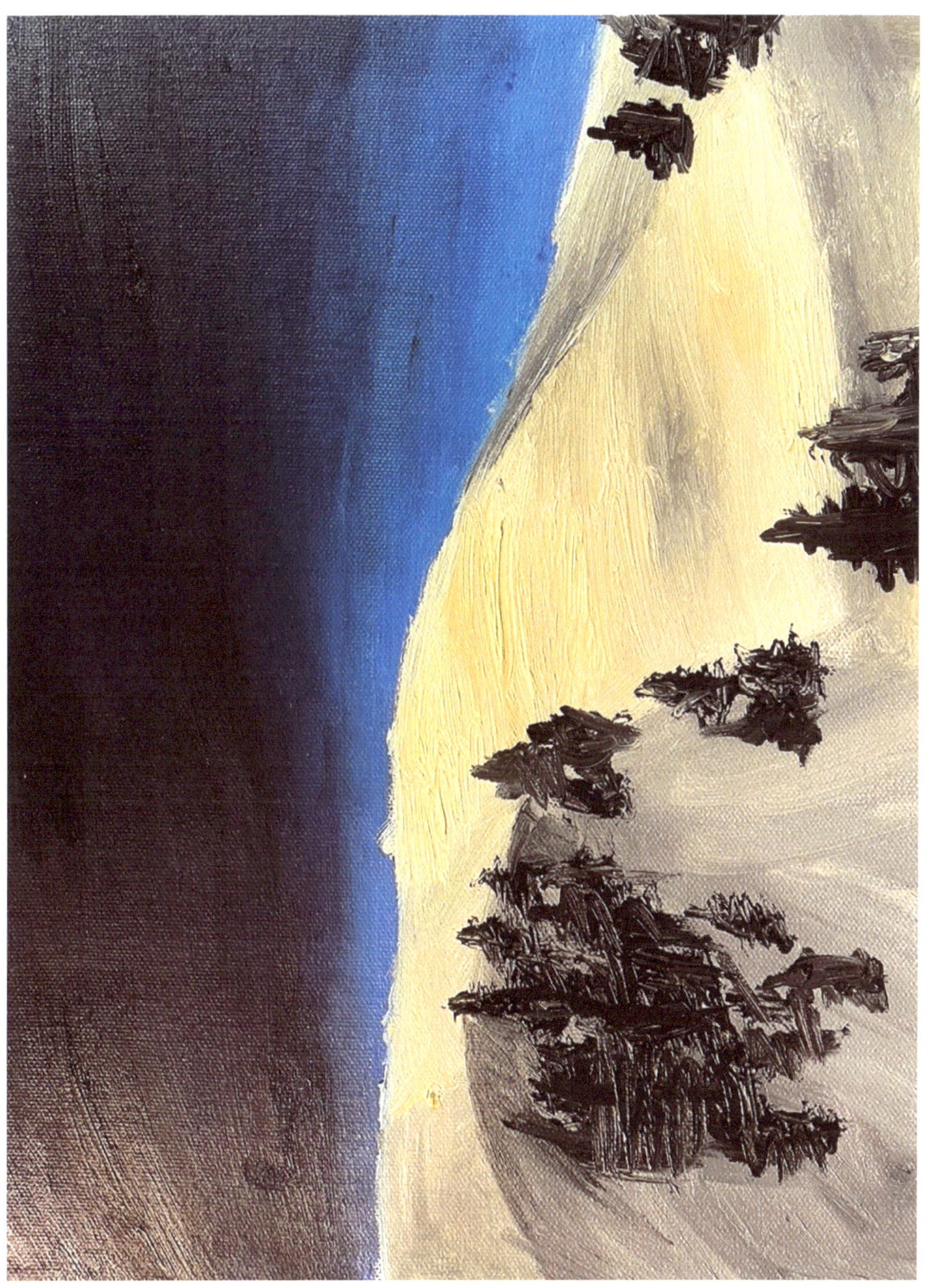

Golden Slope

ELENA LATTERELL

Age 14, West Seattle, WA

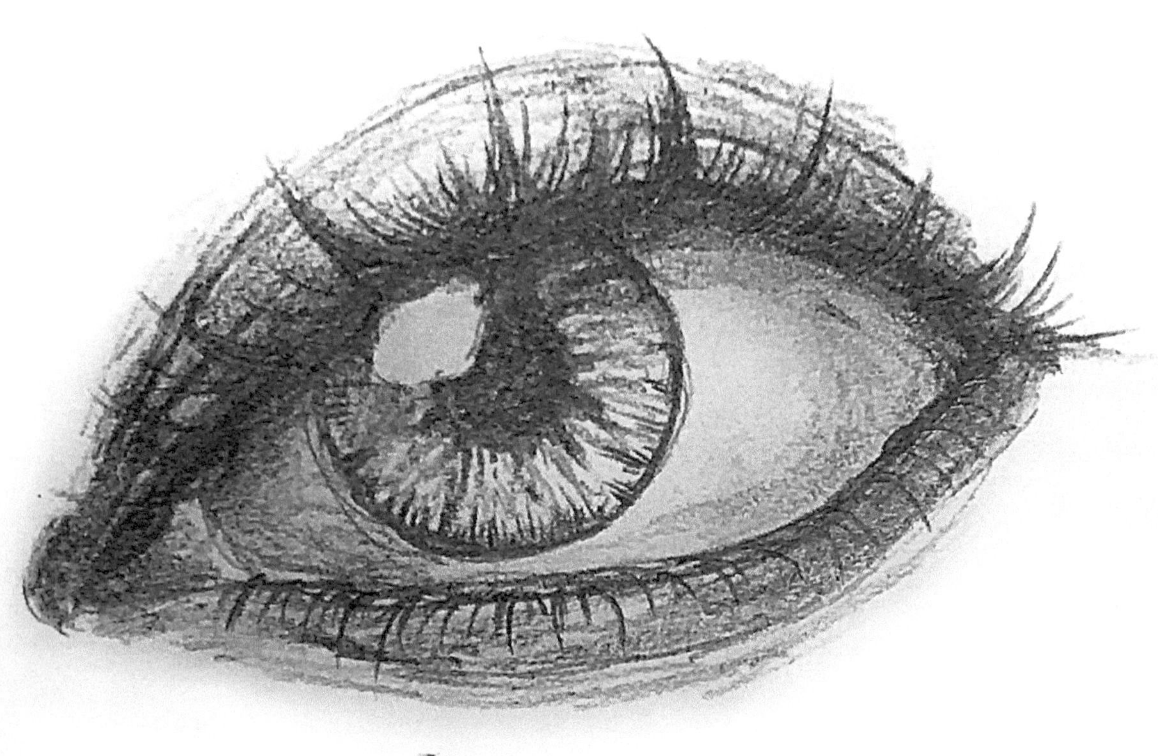

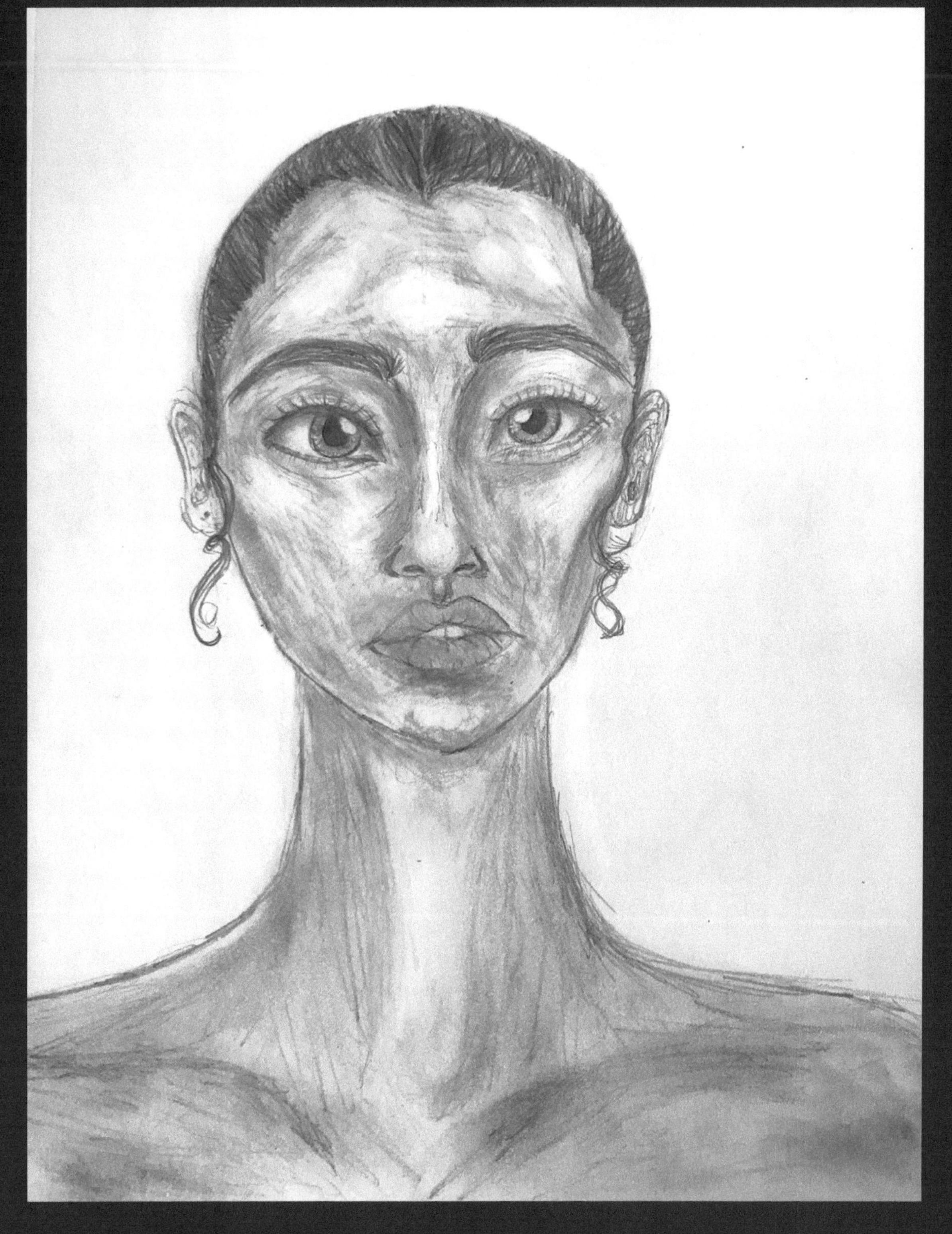

ISABELLA YU

Age 16, Tacoma, WA

His Eyes

We always thought that war seemed far away from us.
Within the pages of some ancient chapter,
Long since lost to time,

I gazed deep into his eyes.
Through the reflection of his eyes,
I see the other side of the world.

Blustery wind like the tip of a callous blade,
Tearing at the heart with a roar of fury.
Hollowing fiercely as if it could bring the innocent soul
Back from the Lethe.
Attempting to revive the earth
That slumbers under the blood.

A steady stream of bodies has long since silenced
The cries for aid.
Blessing faithfully with all my devotion.
Praying that peace would one day arrive.

Beneath the bushy eyebrows lie a pair of stewing eyes
Full of boundless childlike innocence.
It lingers in my mind and cannot be erased.

His eyes remain unclouded, even by the blaze of battle.
All along, I had the sensation that
This wasn't going to be his intended destination.

Then I recognize
There are no winners in war, only losers.
The loss is inconsistently distributed.

He stares back at me.
And down came the rain on my aching heart.
I heard lullabies with lyrical strings.
The vibrant flowers and chirping birds fill my nose.
I could see the hum of happiness and laughter.

I want him to feel it as well.
I hope that by looking into my eyes,
He will see beyond the imprisonment of war.

The dove of peace will eventually cross the Atlantic
And land on the stained shore
Recounting the next chapter with hope.

ELLEN HEACOCK

Age 15, Tacoma, WA

**"Будь ласка, залишайтеся в безпеці
та теплі. Світ підтримує Україну."**

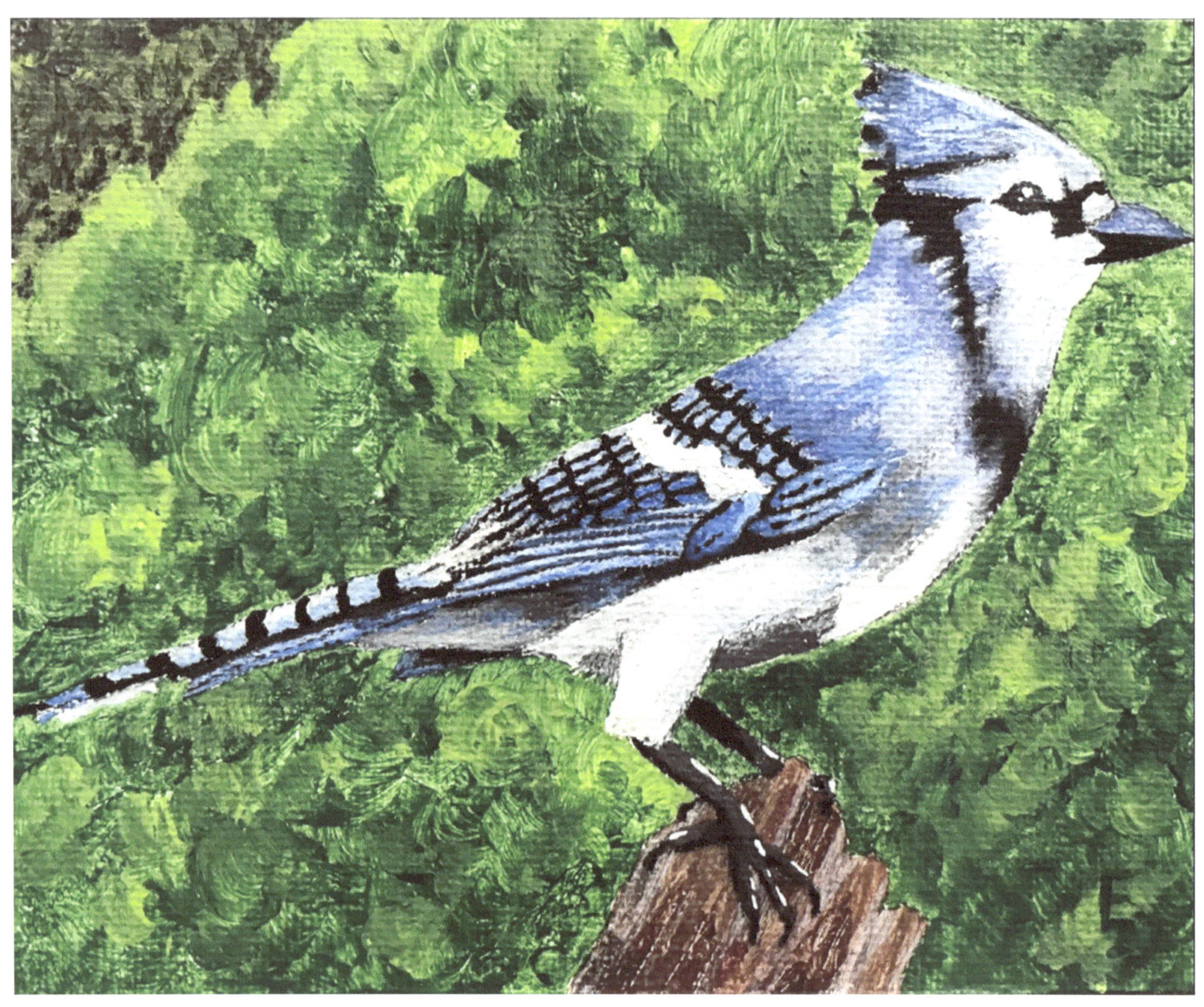

**Please stay safe and warm.
The world supports Ukraine.**

"Не здавайтеся, будь ласка, знайте, що вас люблять і про вас піклуються, навіть якщо ви почуваєтеся самотніми. Будь мужнім. Слава Україні!"

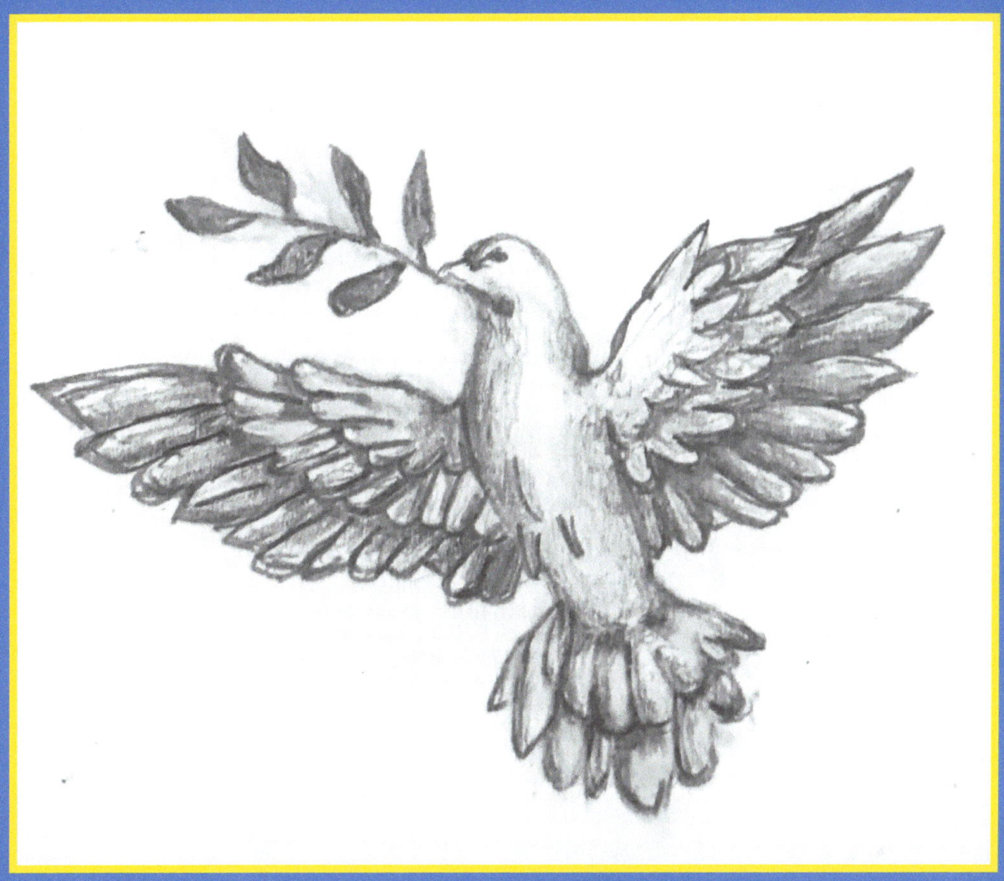

Don't give up, please know that you are loved and cared for even if you feel alone. Be courageous. Glory to Ukraine!

CHLOE CHEN

Age 17, Tacoma, WA

A Hug

I call security a hug, or peace away from the war.

I don't need mountains of jewels and fame like that,
I just want the safety of my family.
I never wish to travel around world
or dine at a luxury restaurant,
I only long for a chance to go to school
and for a meal made by my mom.

But I am hungry, and I lost my mom.

Dust littered my world from birth, dirt and dust
became symbols that I could not wash away.
Even the people who spoke up for me touched dirt
under my eyes to make me look more worthy of pity.

But I don't need pity, I need respect.

Please treat me like a human being,
even if it just allows me to live.
Please treat me like a human being,
even if it just lets my mother come home.

Please give me back the peace I never had,   the peace I once had?
the peace that stood in the world for so long.
Please let me sleep well, with a dry bed
and a sheltered roof.

Please give me a hug, a clean and warm hug.

AHAVA DOLPHA ODABASHIAN

Age 7, NY, NY

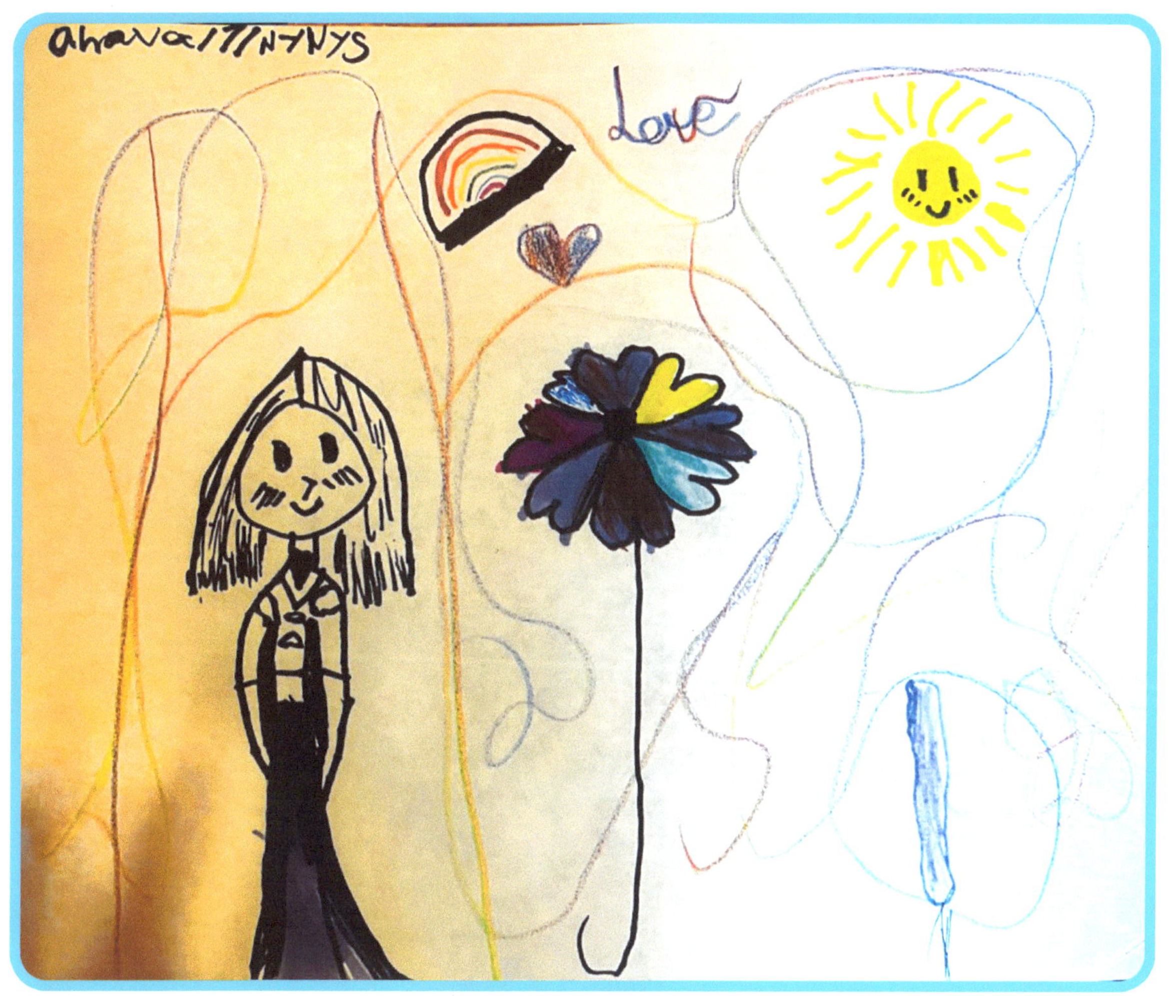

JULIA ROSENBERG

Age: 10, Seattle, WA

caratoe

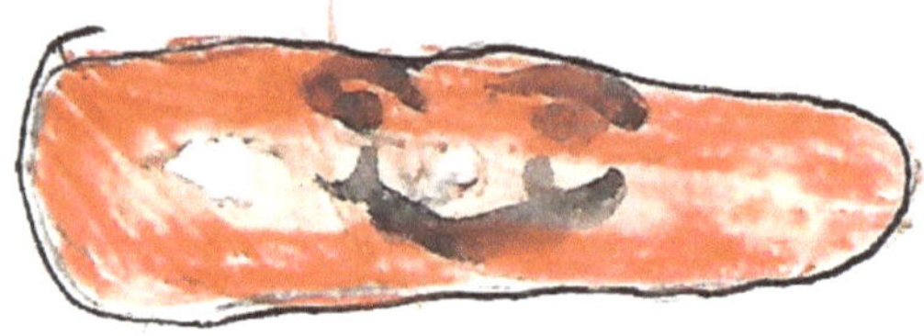

Peaatoe

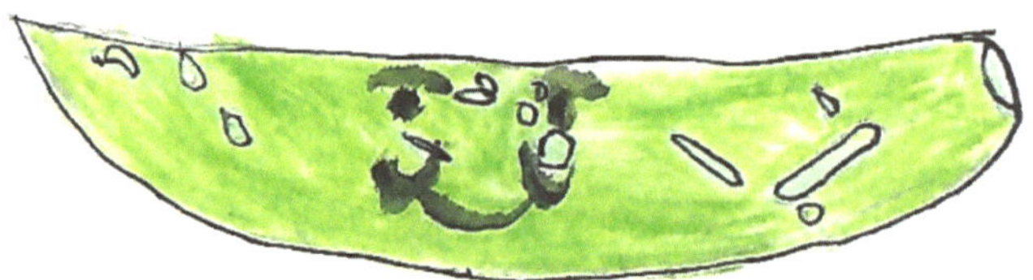

LUKE LINNEMANN

Age 6, Issaquah, WA

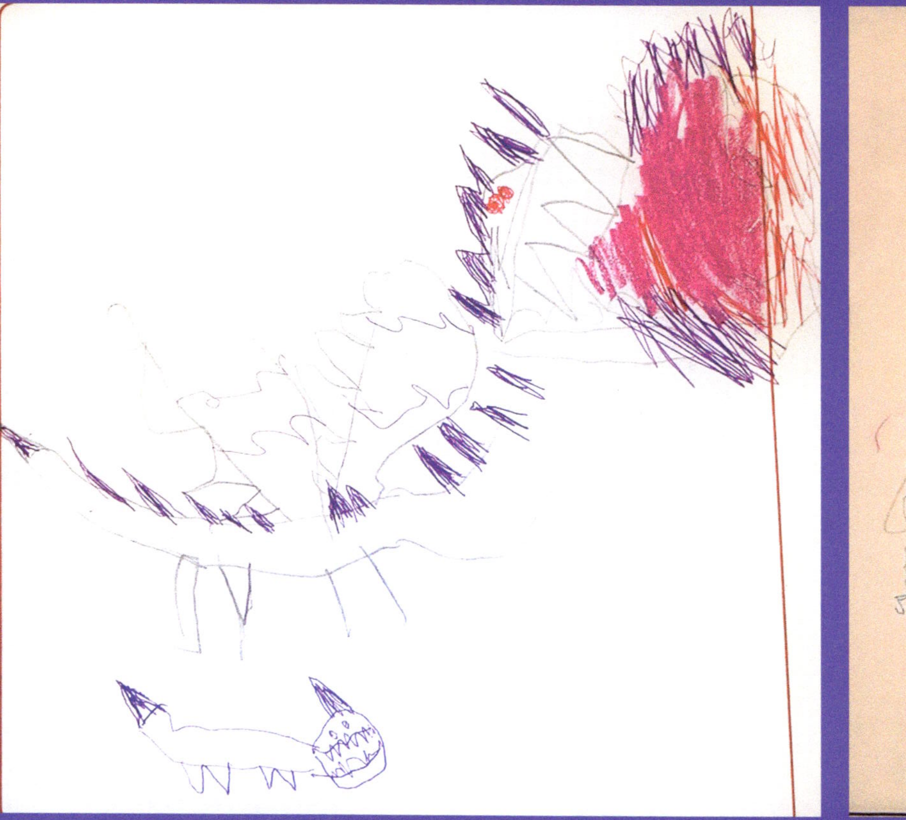

"Dragon and a baby dragon dog"

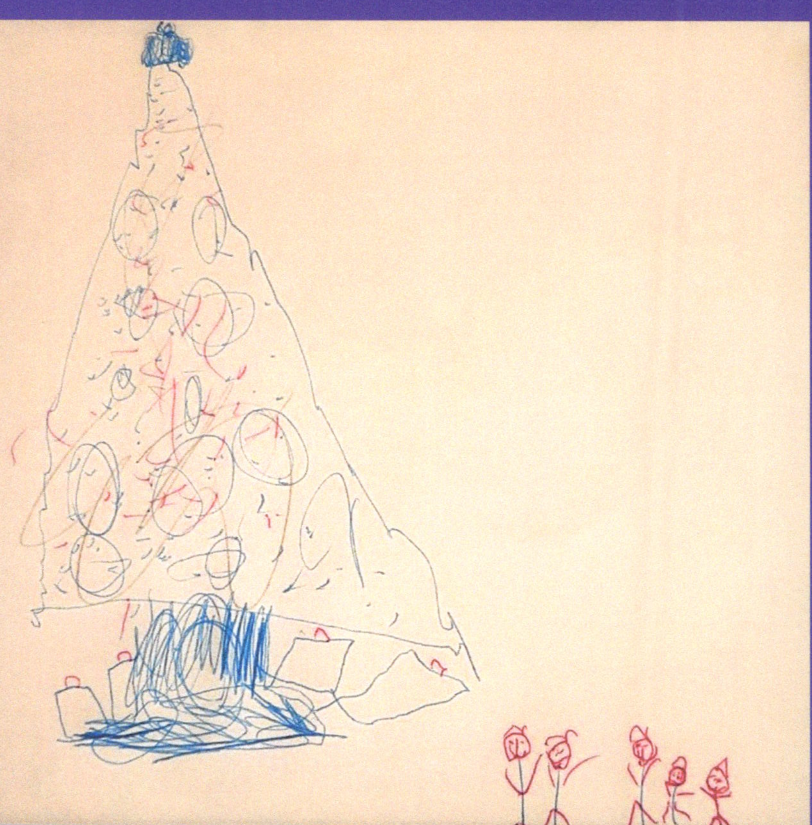

"Christmas Tree. The gifts have Japanese airplanes."

CEDAR SKILLMAN

Age 6, San Francisco, CA

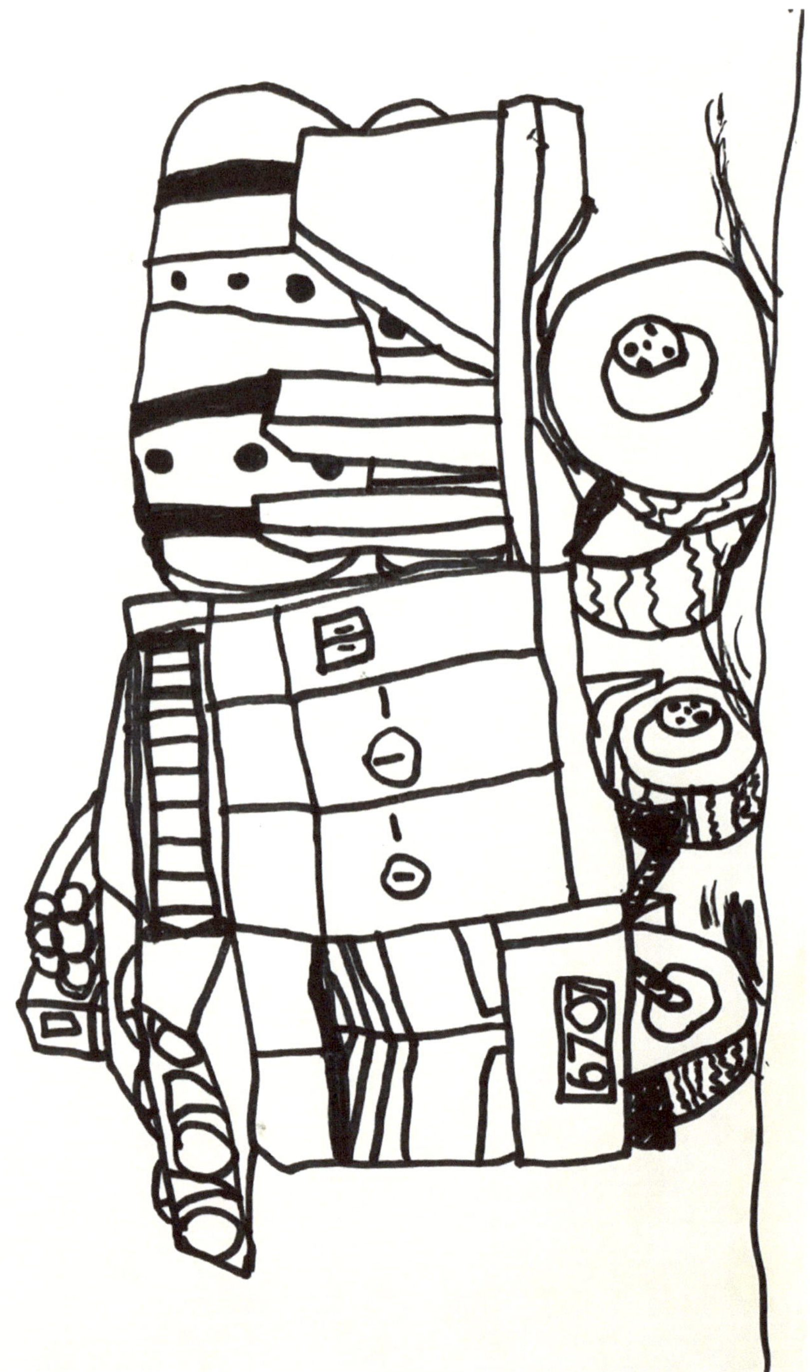

"tanker truck"

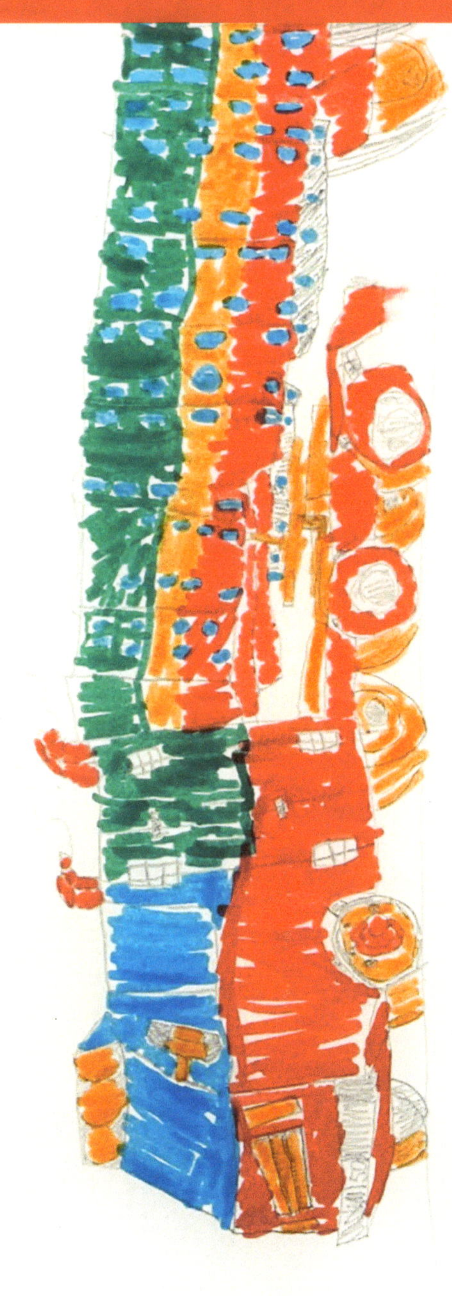

OLYMPIA WADDEN

Age 13, West Seattle, WA

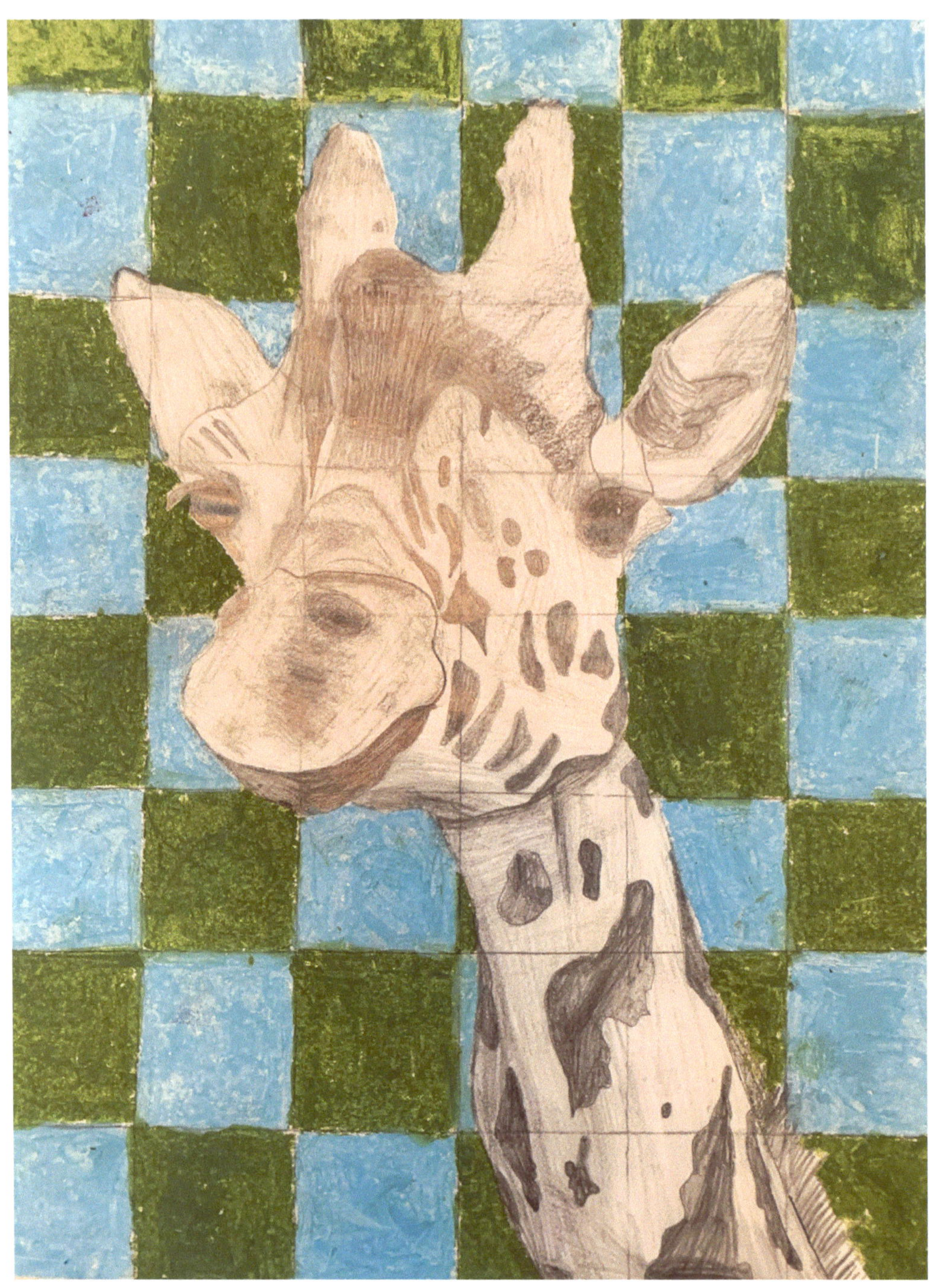

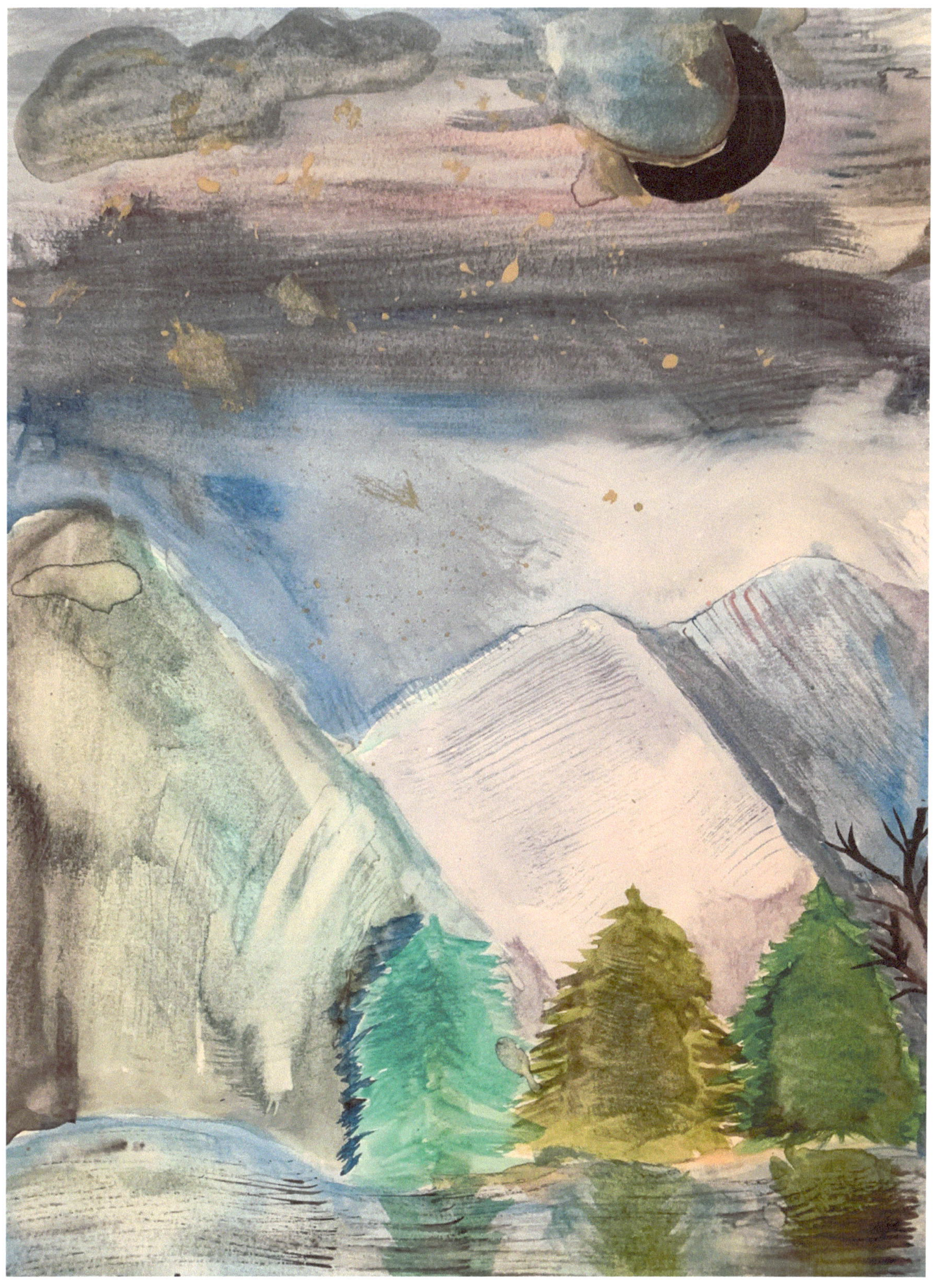

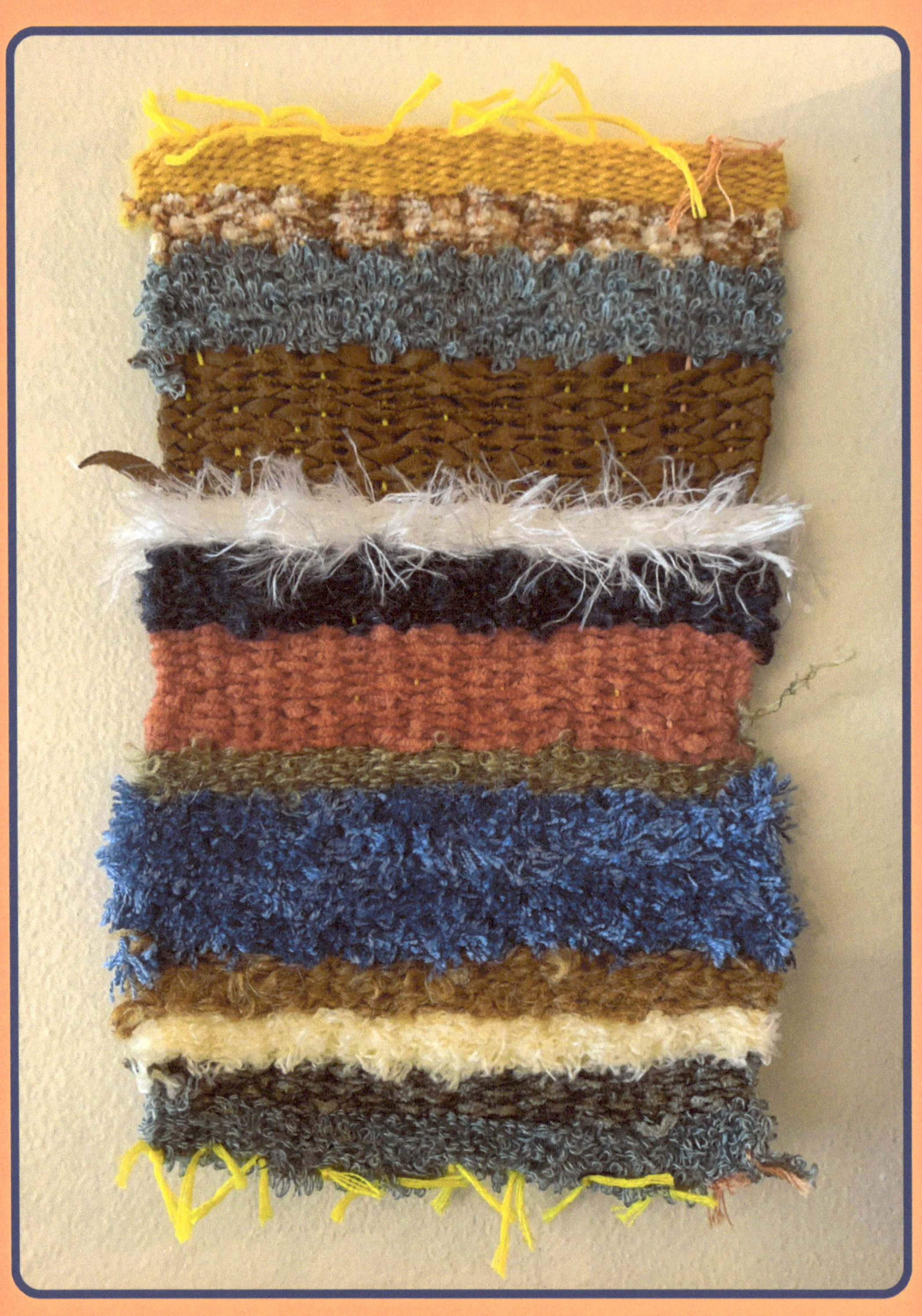

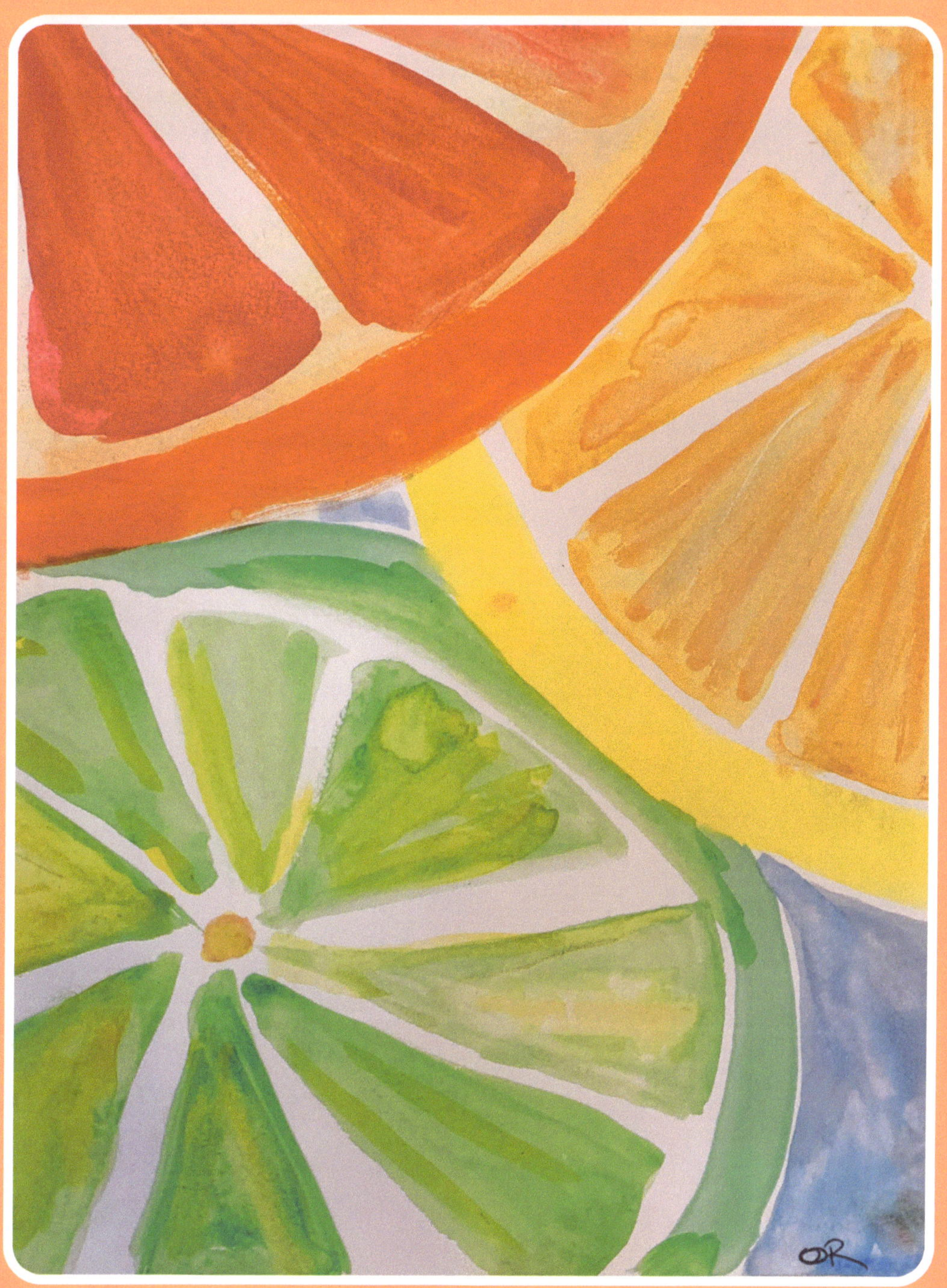

TOMO K. BERGMAN

Age 9, Seattle, Washington

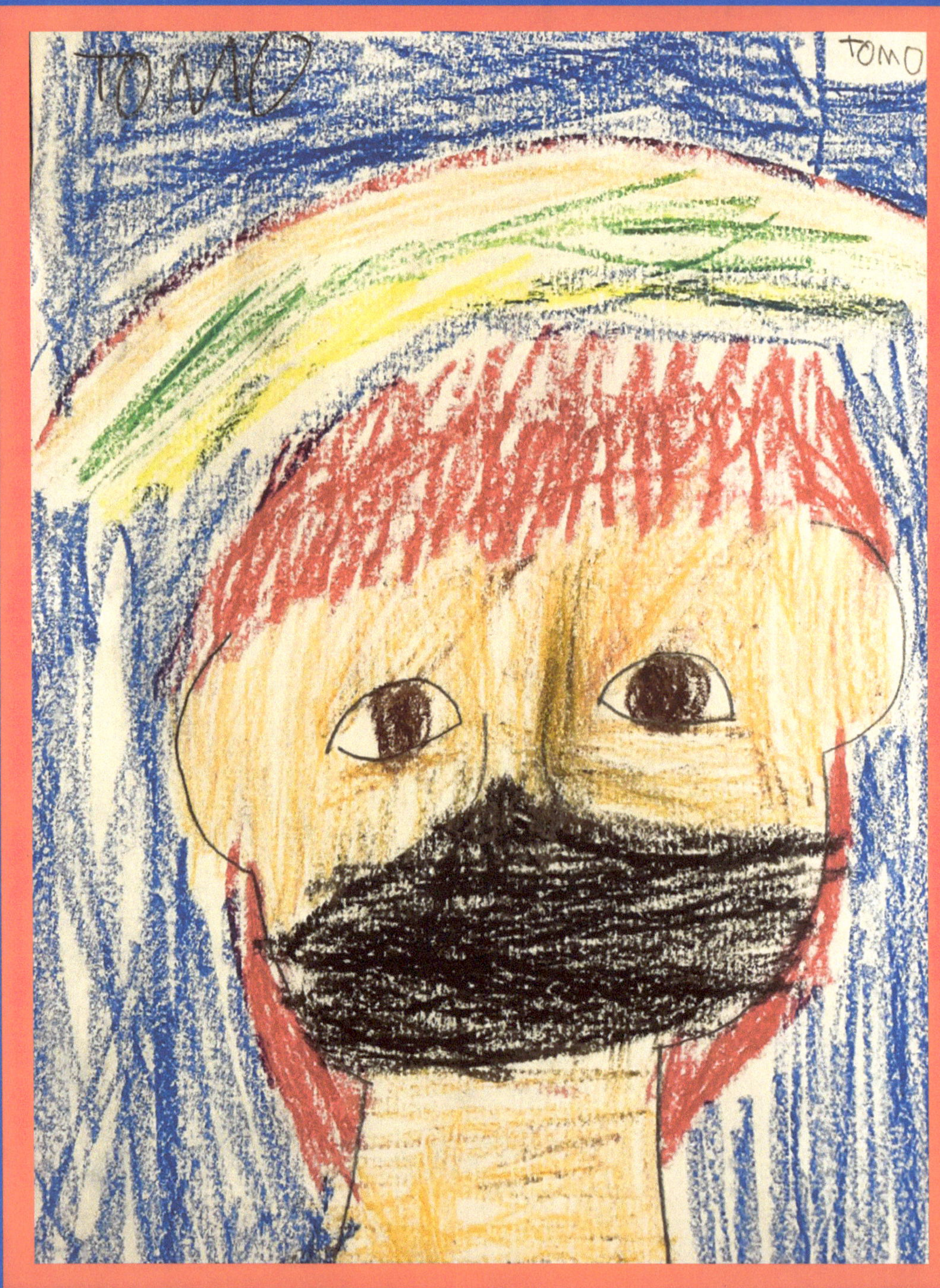

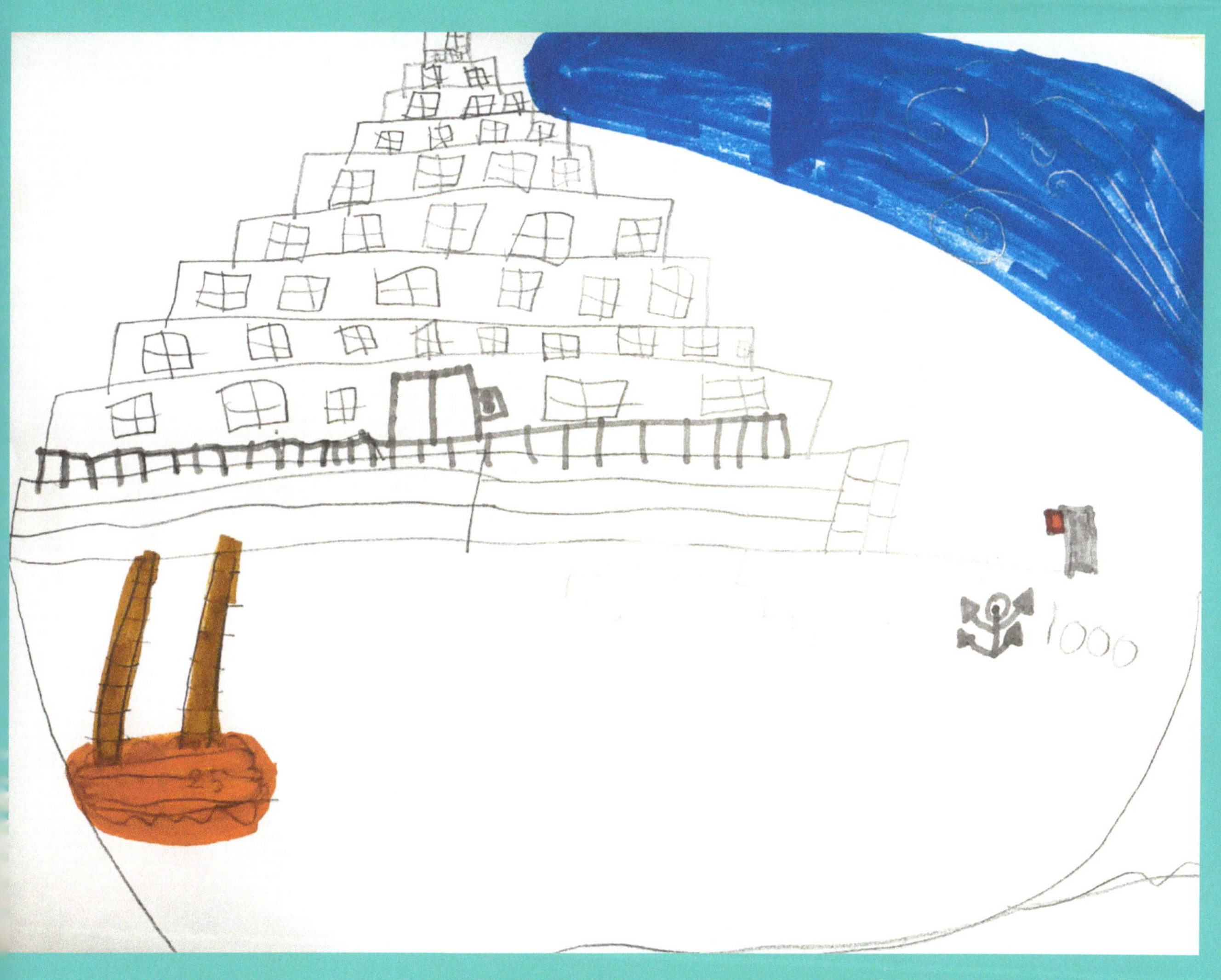

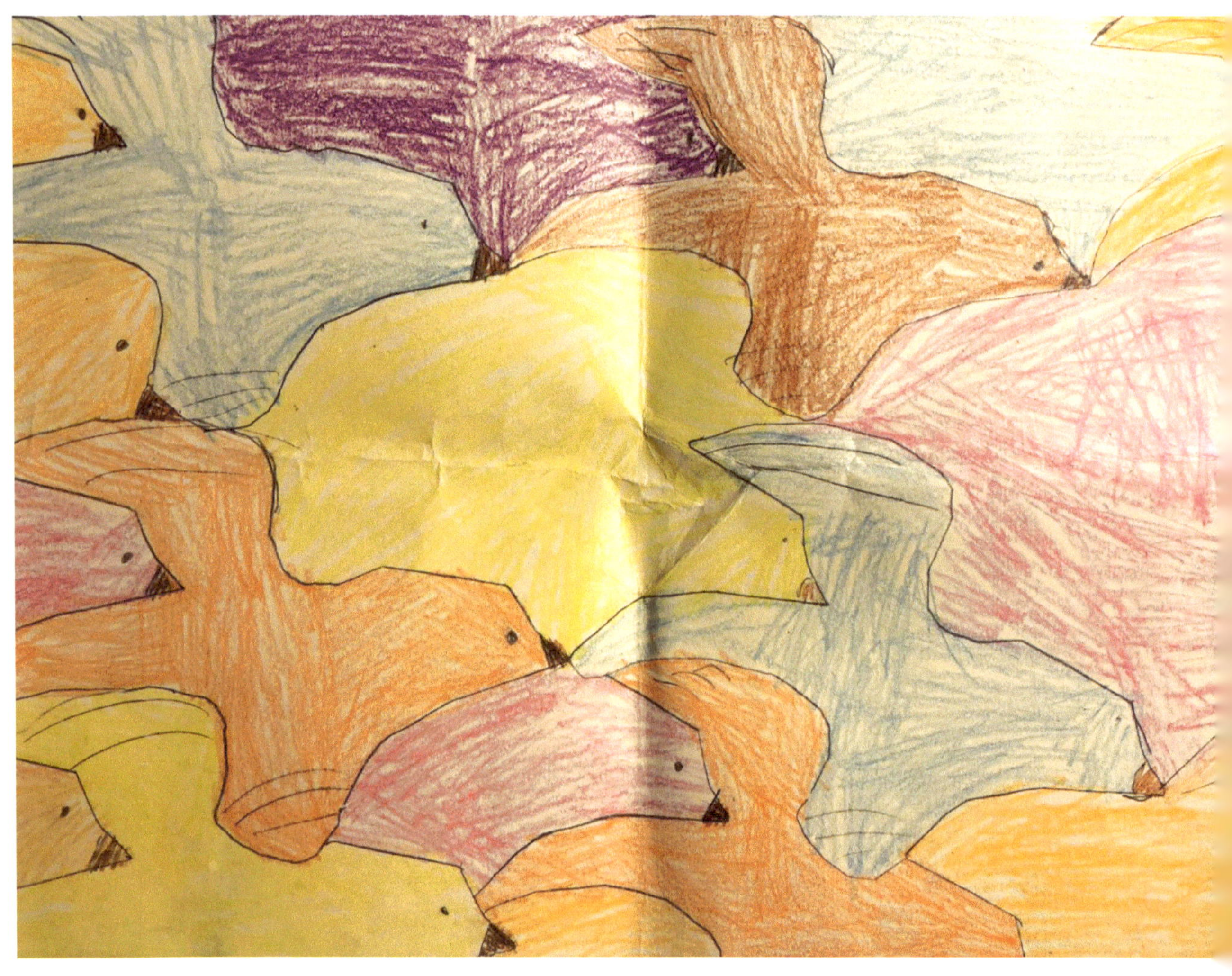

HAZEL TUININGA

Age 15, North Bend, WA

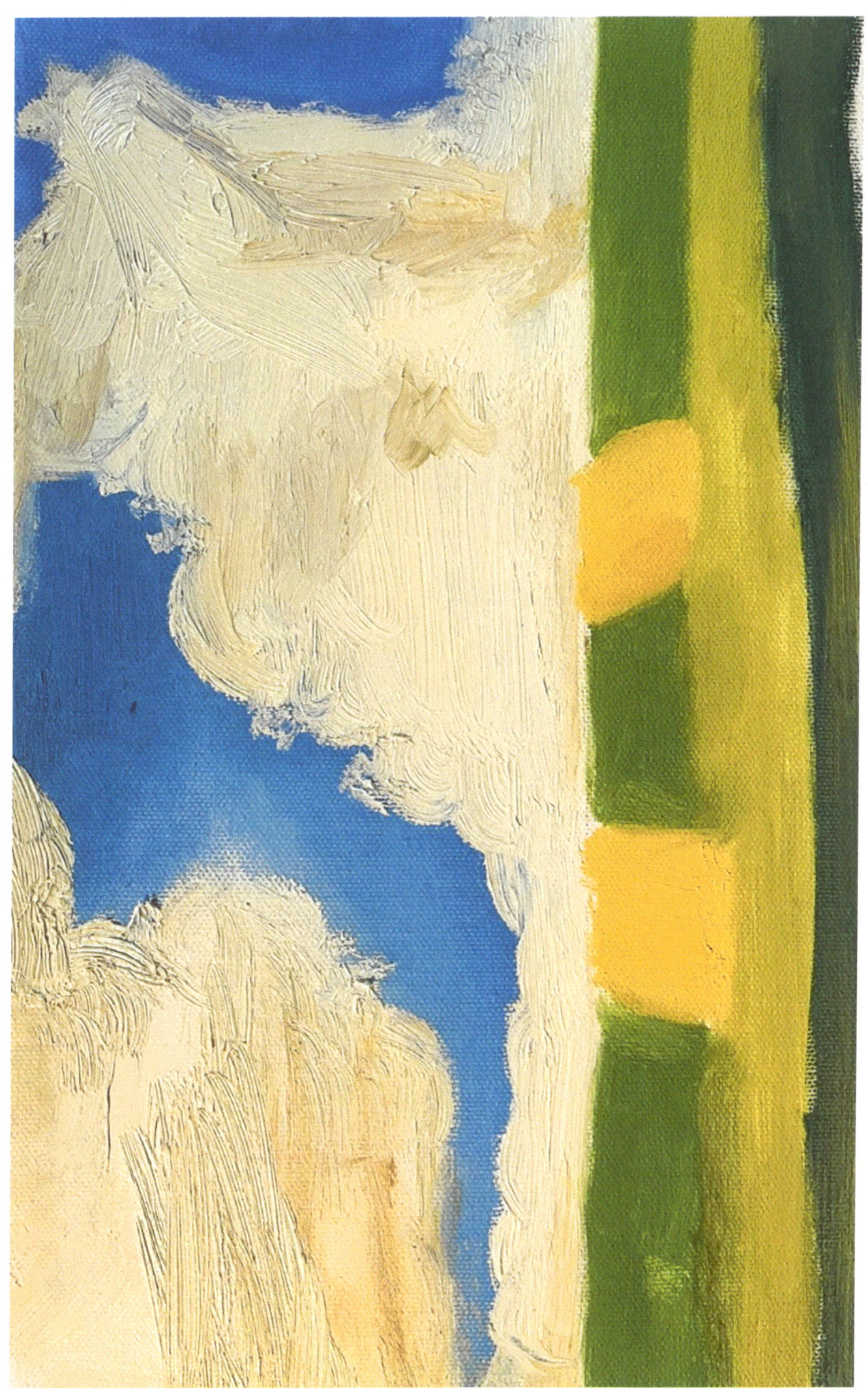

Field & Sky

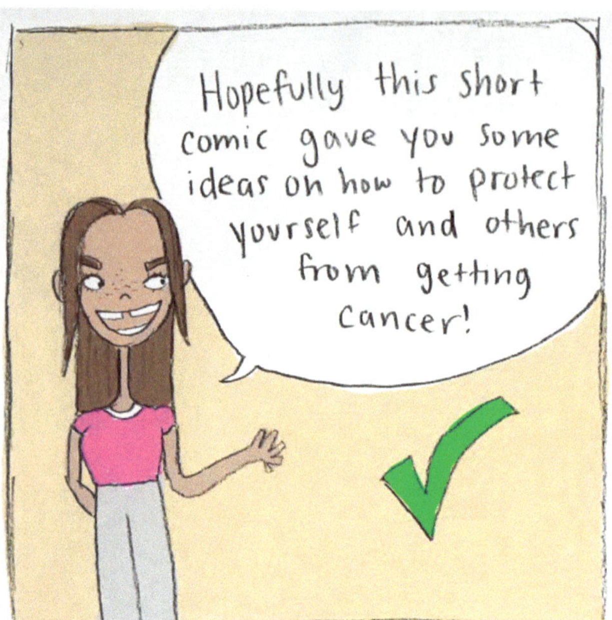

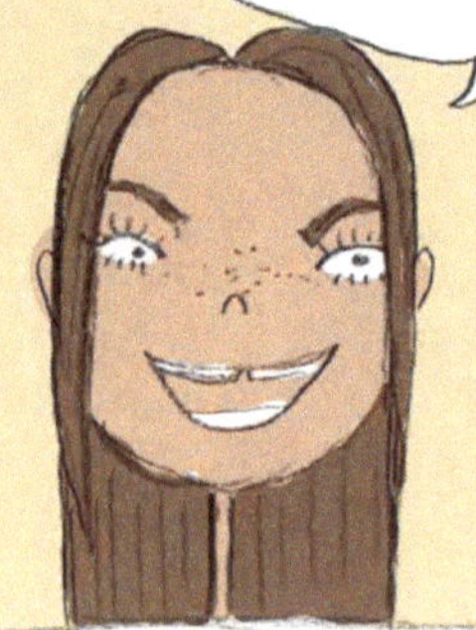

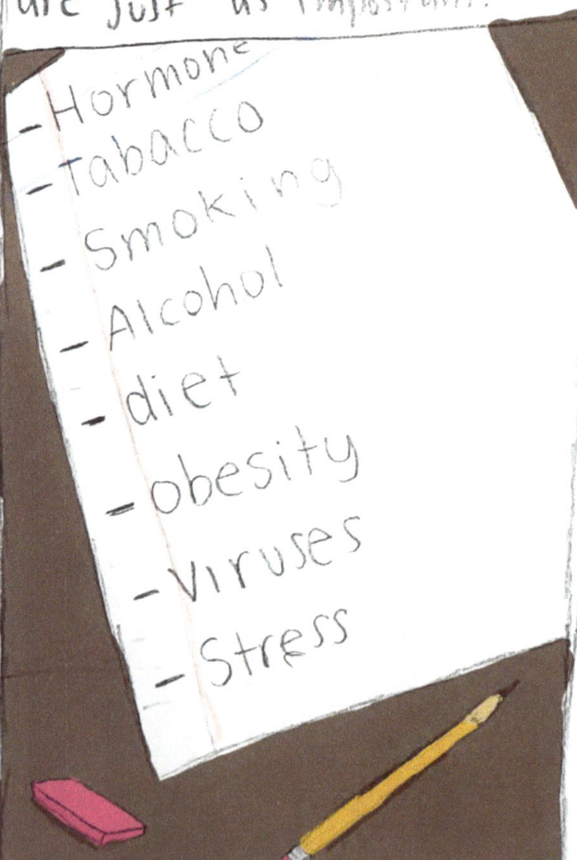

comic By: Hazel Tuininga.

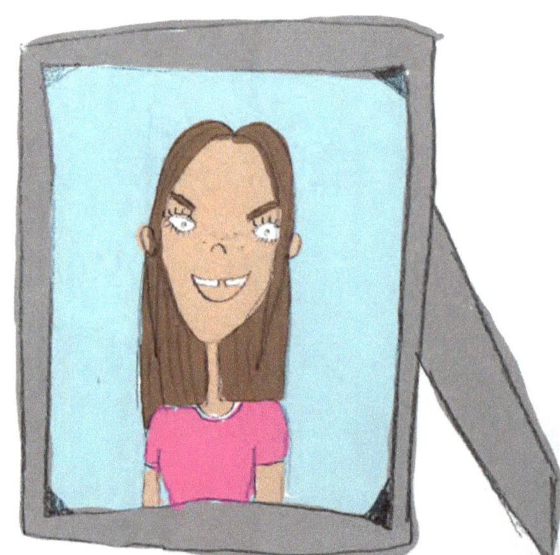

Sources: Spohn Erik 'Inheratence reading." Spohn Erik "Skin cancer background. Spohn Erik "cancer risk factors. 12 lessons learned from Mr. Spohns freshman biology class including Readings, class notes, and videos.

made on pro create, digital app

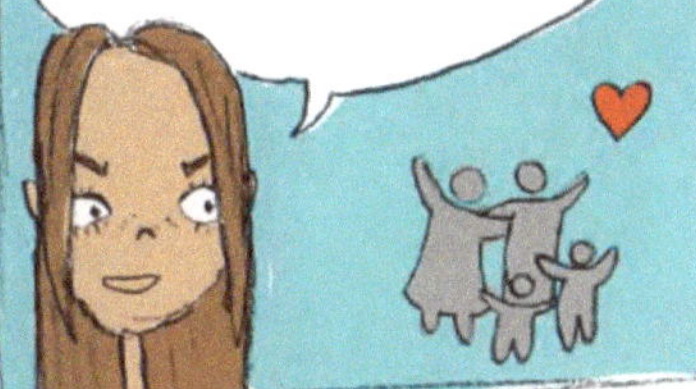
An important thing to know is that cancer can be passed down from families.

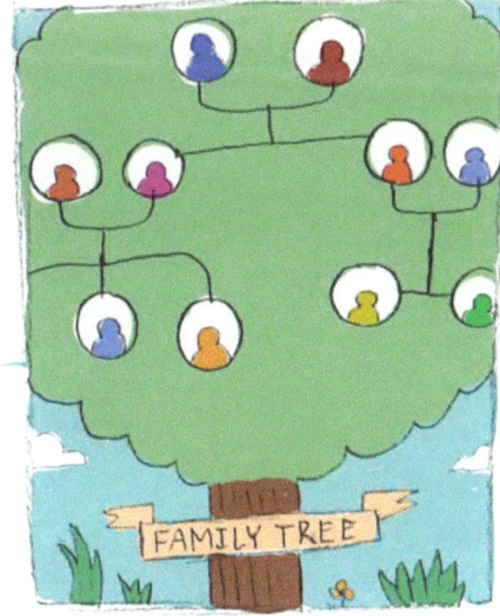
FAMILY TREE

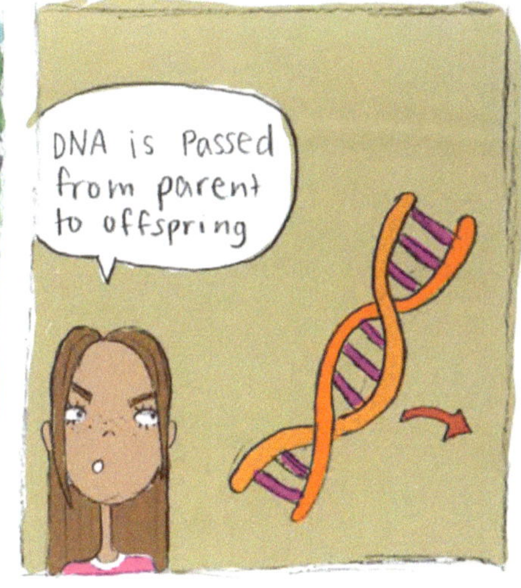
DNA is passed from parent to offspring

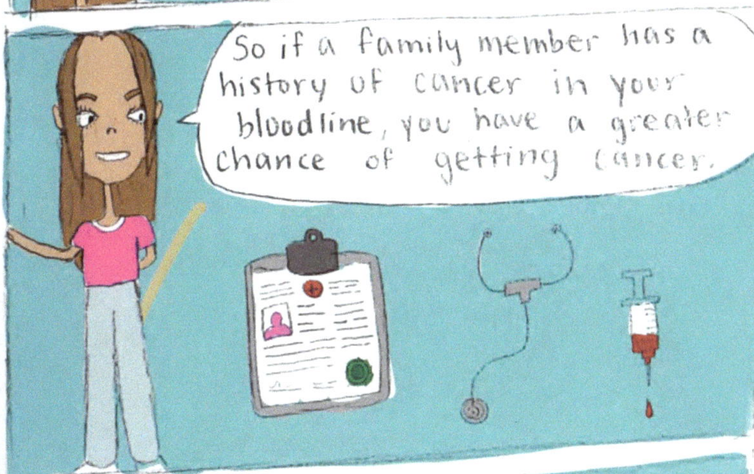
So if a family member has a history of cancer in your bloodline, you have a greater chance of getting cancer.

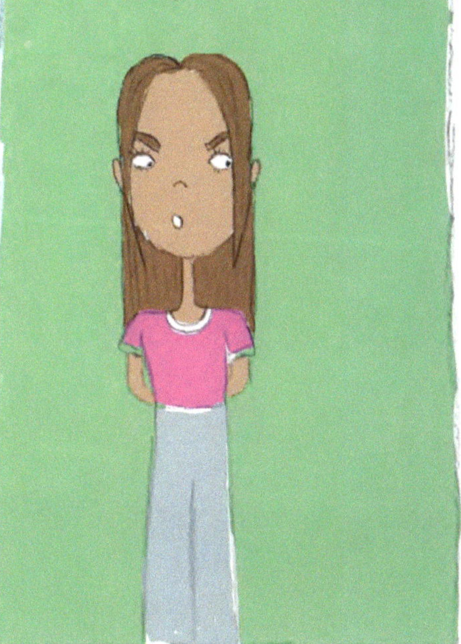
So this means that some parents could not have cancer but still pass it on to other generations

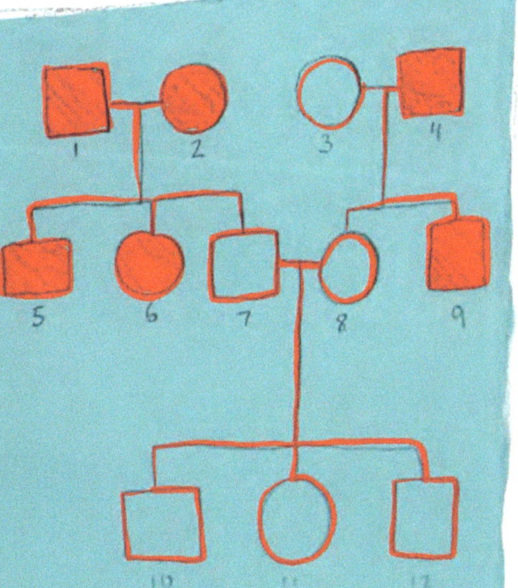
Another thing to note is that half of your genetic information comes from each parent ...
1
2
3
4
5
6
7
8
9
10
11
12

2nd RISK FACTOR: UV Radiation

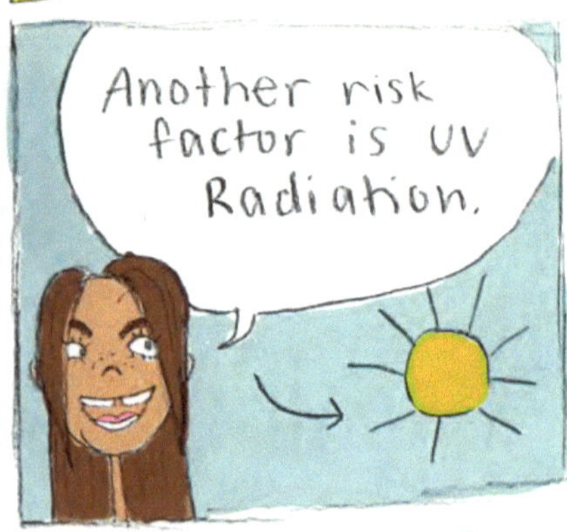

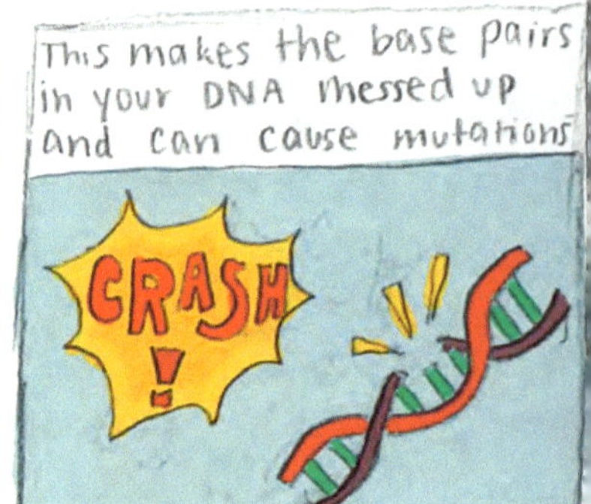

This makes the base pairs in your DNA messed up and can cause mutations

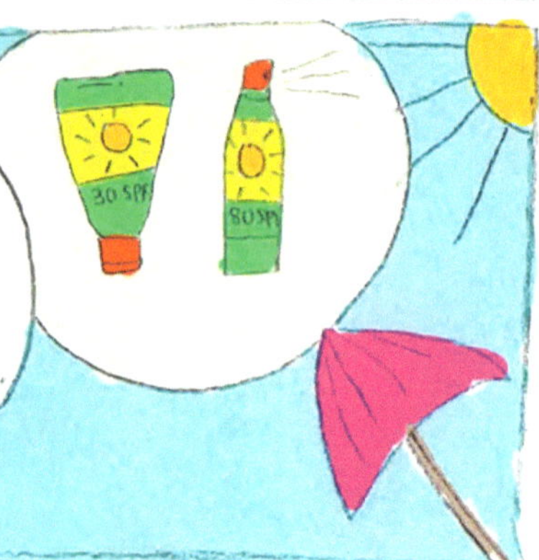

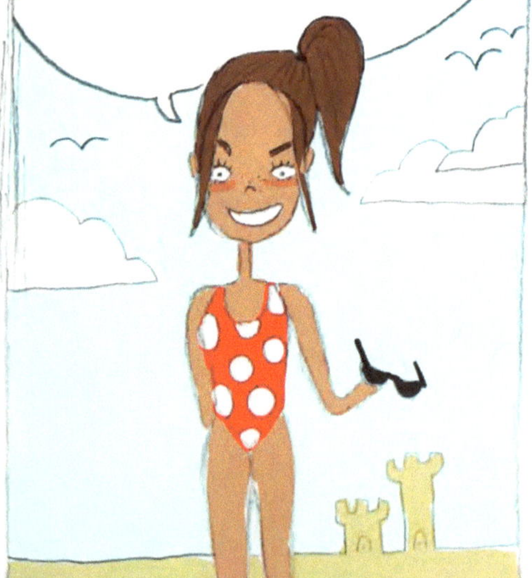

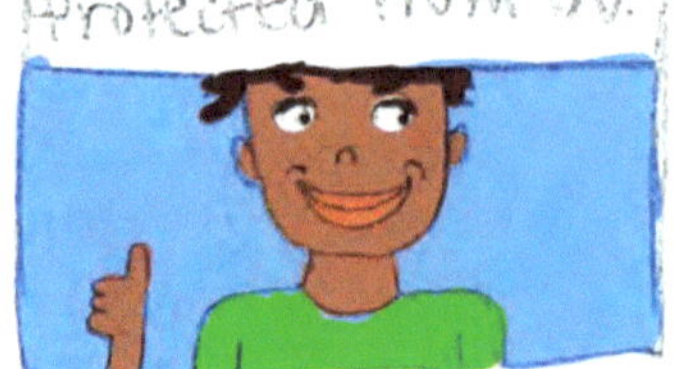

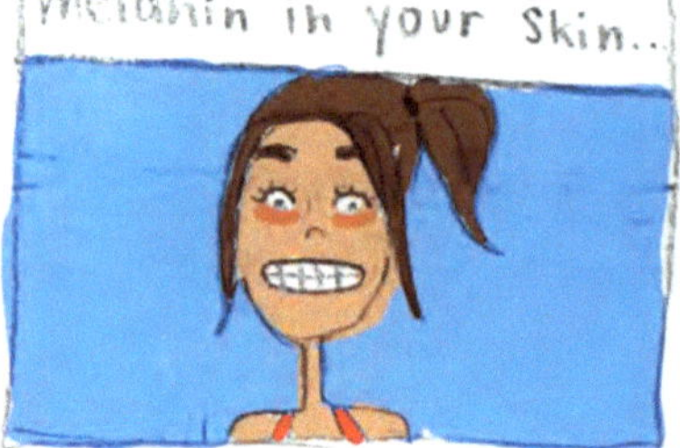

3rd RISK FACTOR: Environment

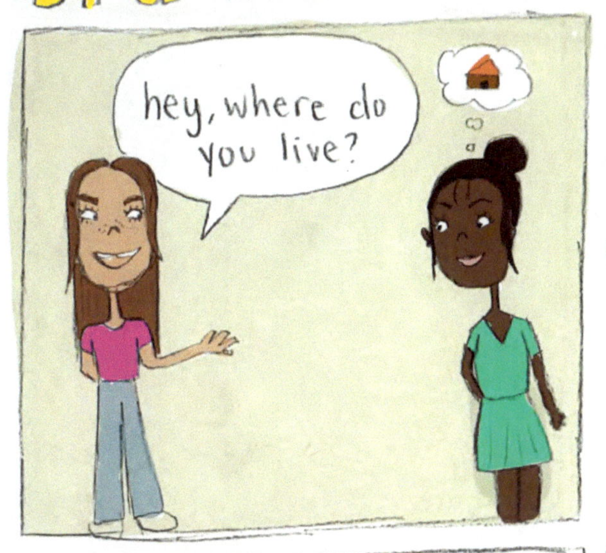

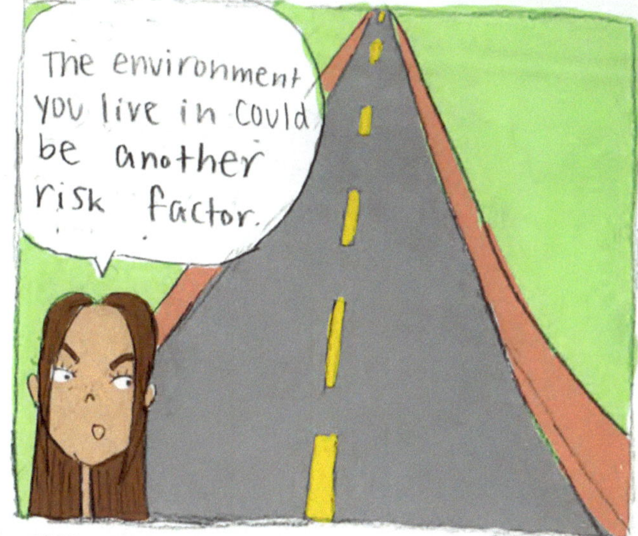

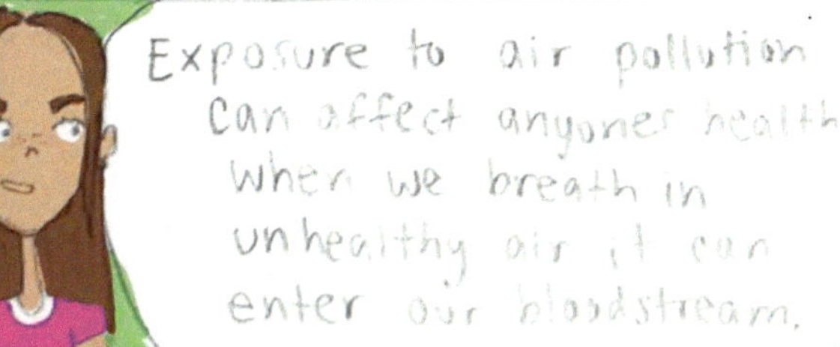

Air pollution is bad for for your lungs and heart health and increases risks of breast cancer in the chest.

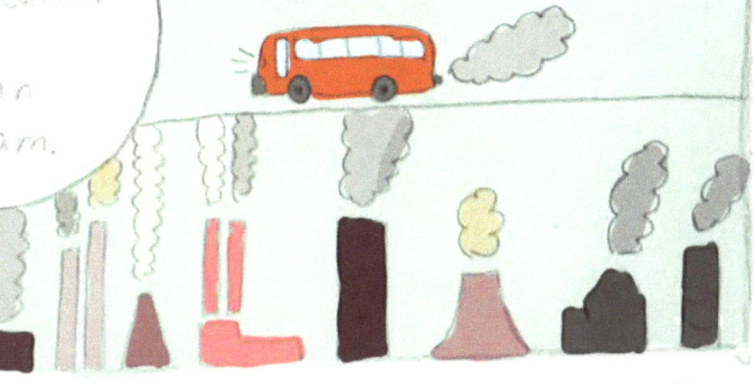

4th RISK FACTOR: YOUR HEIGHT AND AGE

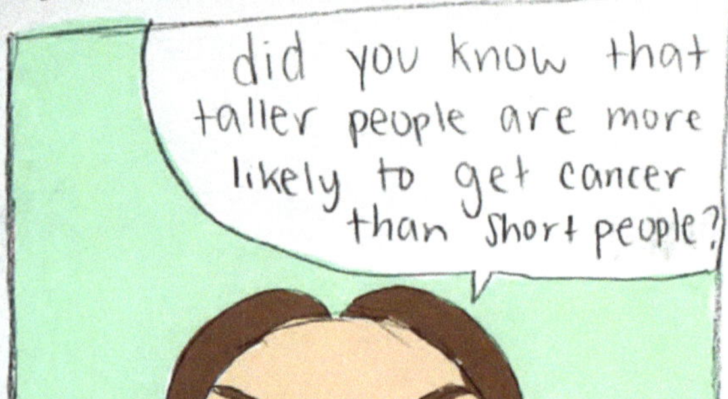

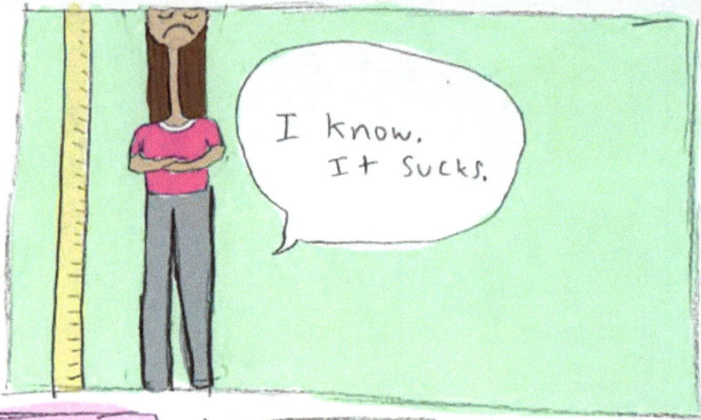

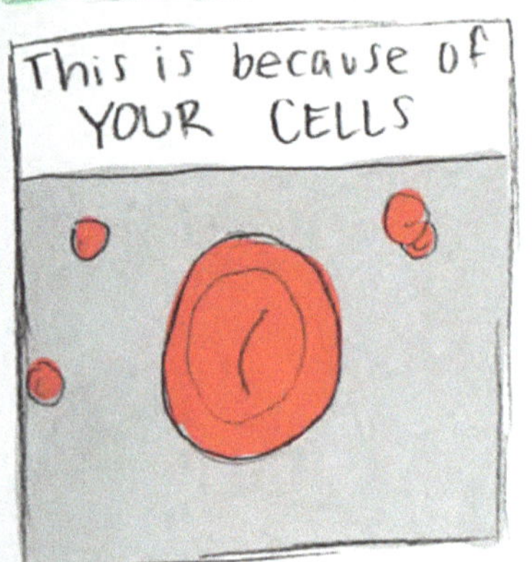

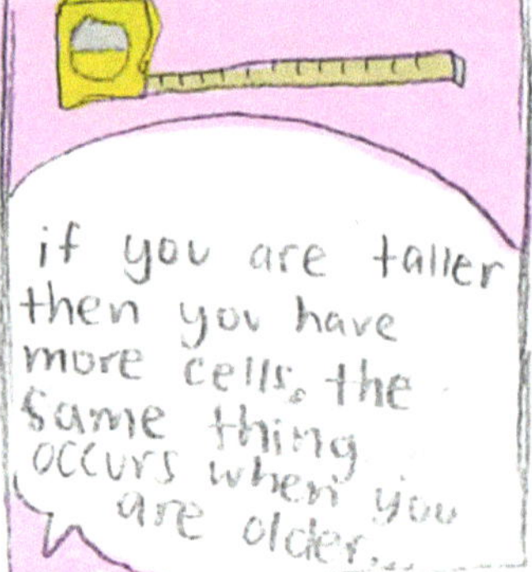

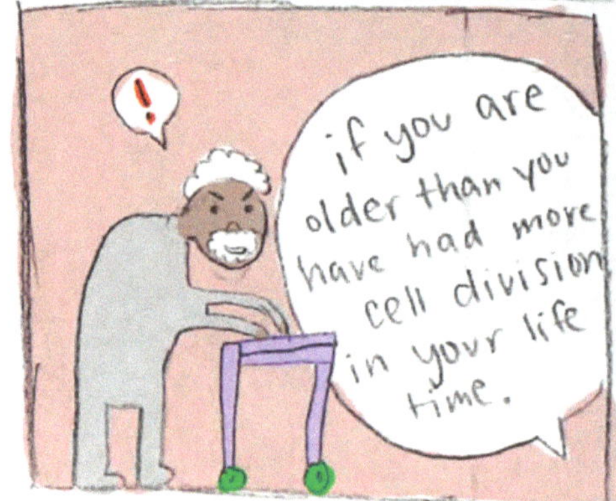

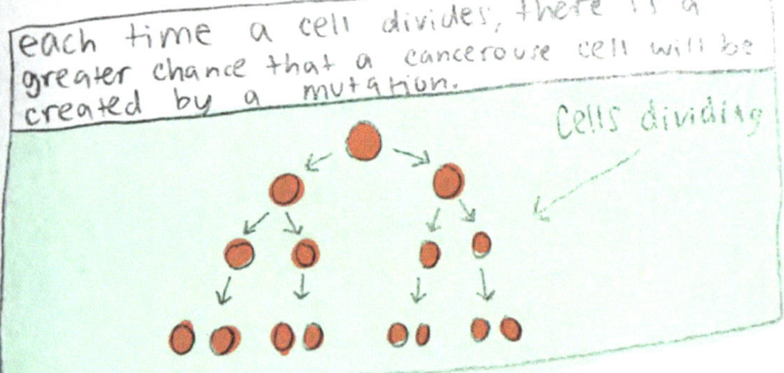

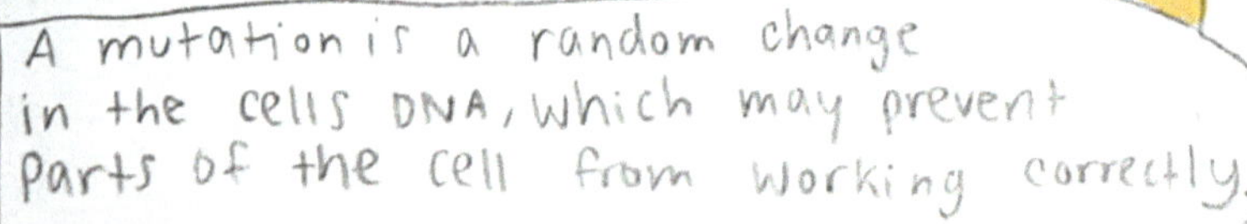

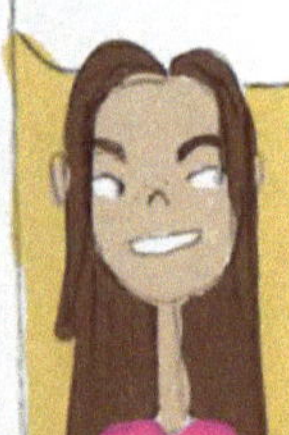

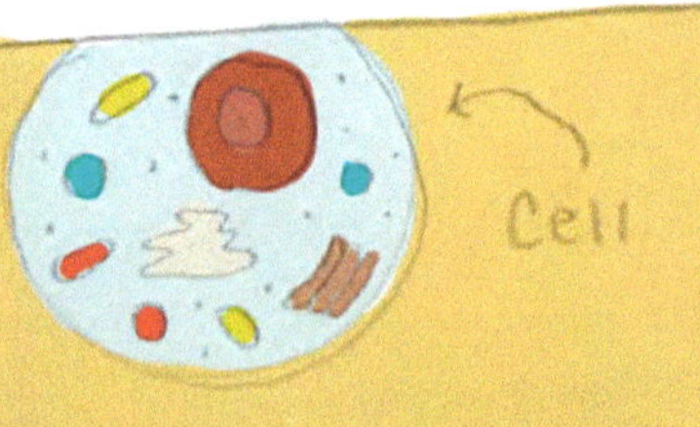

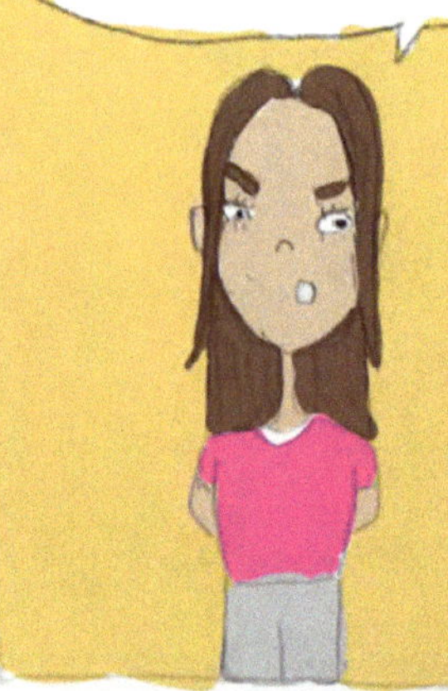

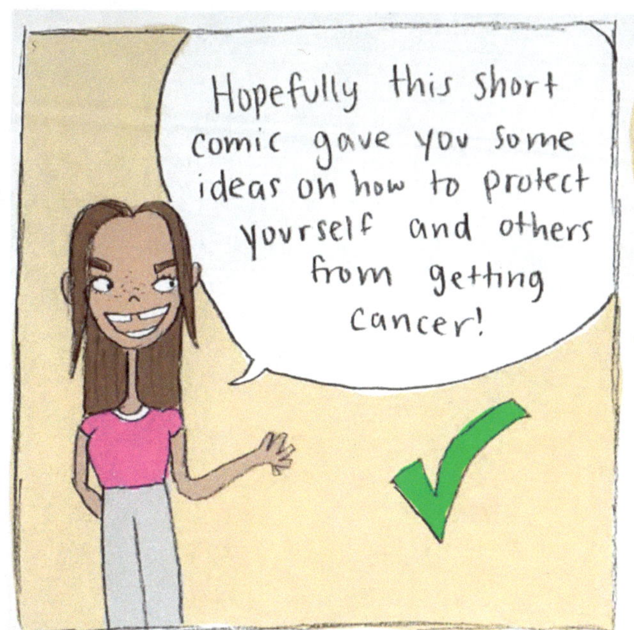

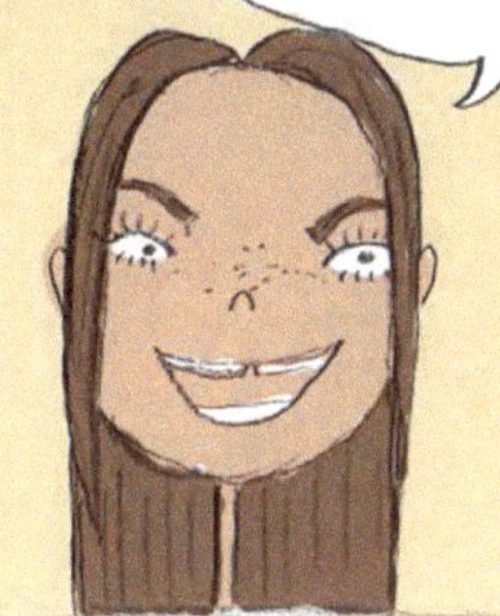

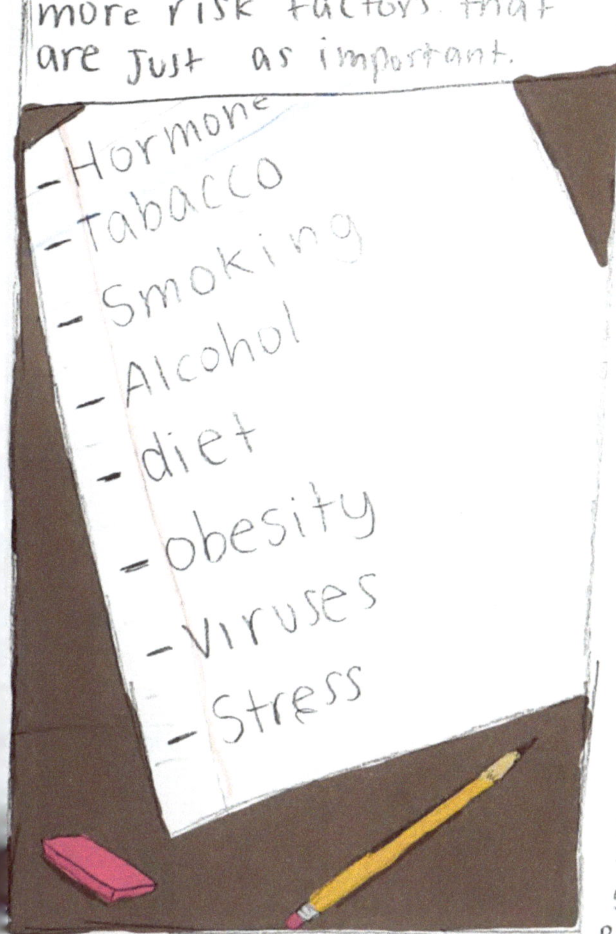

Comic By: Hazel Tuininga.

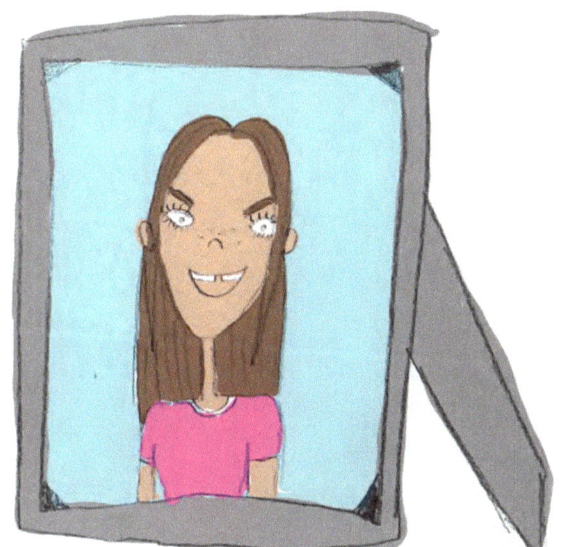

LIANA MACIUKENAS

Age 13, Portland, OR

~ A Little Escape ~

The sea is lapping at my feet drawing me near.
My feet crunch the sand as I walk the U shaped waters.
I watch as a fisherman comes back from sea
The horizon of the sea is beautiful.

The water is as cold as snow
My sweater warms me
The rocks around the beach make a hidden kingdom
The water is as clear as glass.

I am glad I came here, all the way from my house across the highway
The U of water that comes from the ocean is slender but deep
The little saltwater pool is sparkling in the dim moonlight.

My phone rings, I come back to reality
I take one last look at the glistening horizon with the sun slowly waking up
I feel safe here, I don't want to leave, but I can't stay here forever
I lean down and whisper to the waters "I will come back"
And as if it hears me, the water gives a splash of joy.

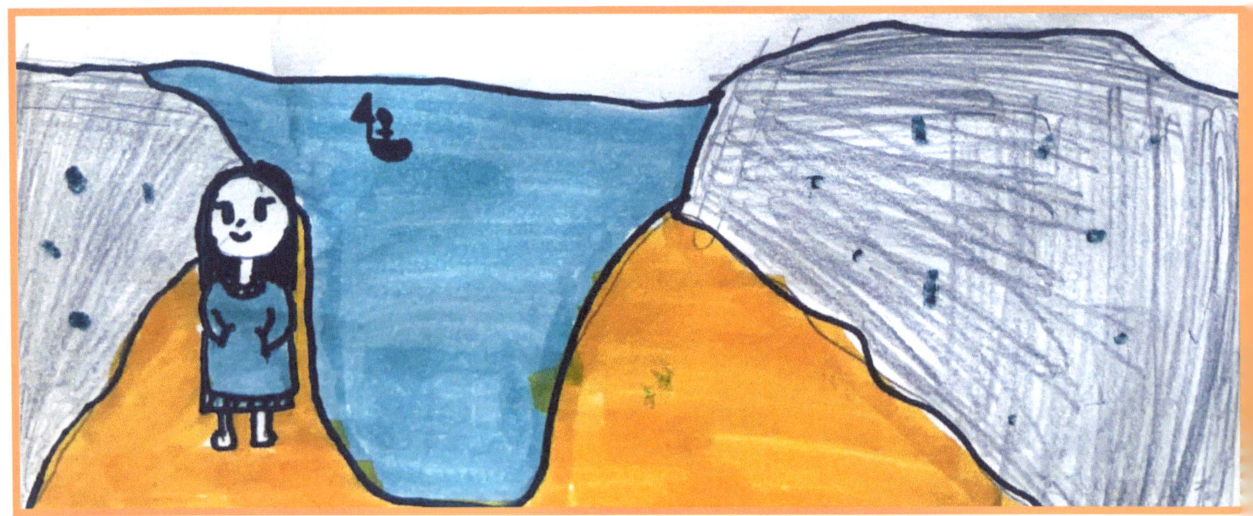

LEO MACIUKENAS

Age 11, Portland, OR

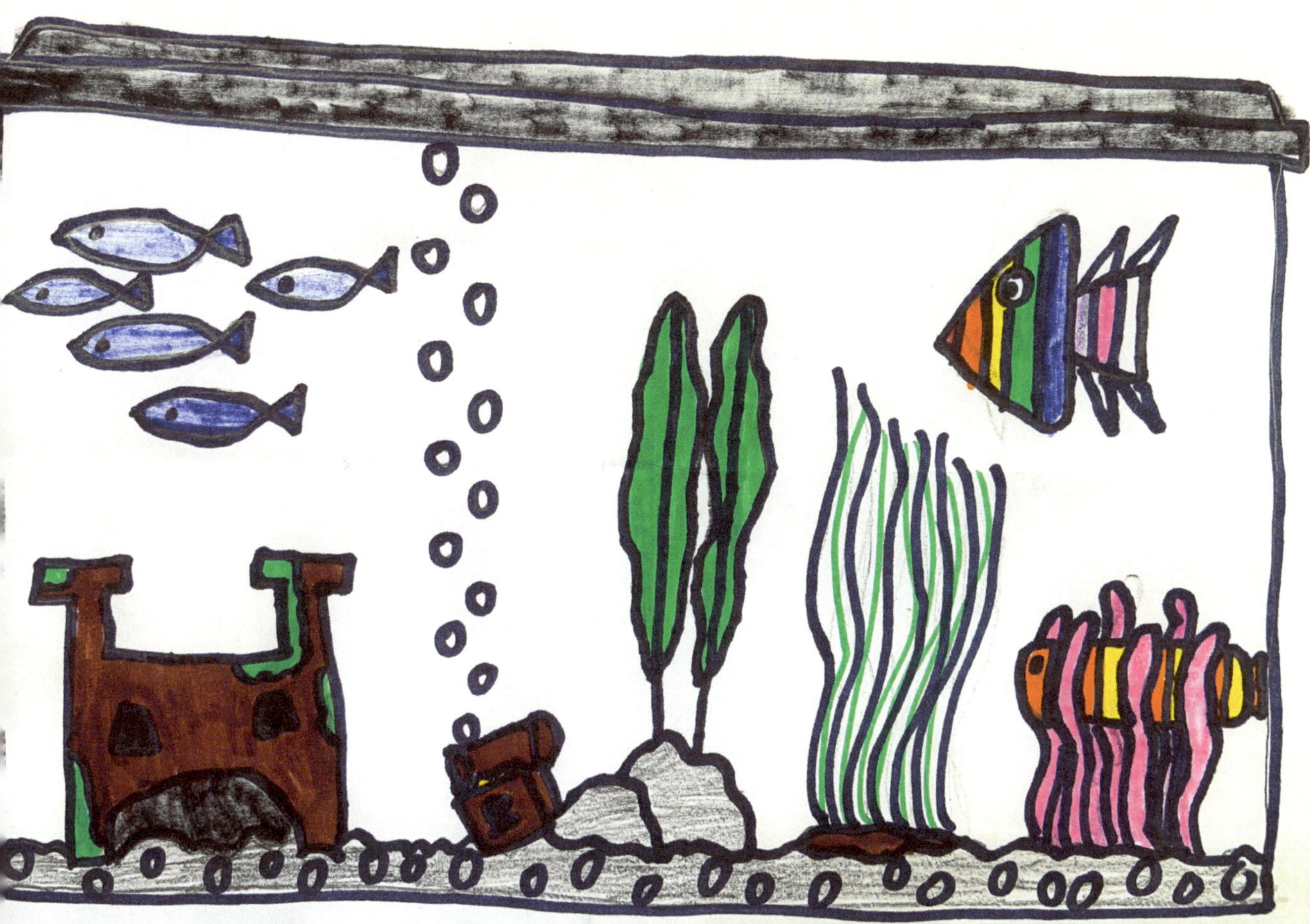

"Colorful Aquarium"

AVERY ZIMMER

Age 16, West Seattle, WA

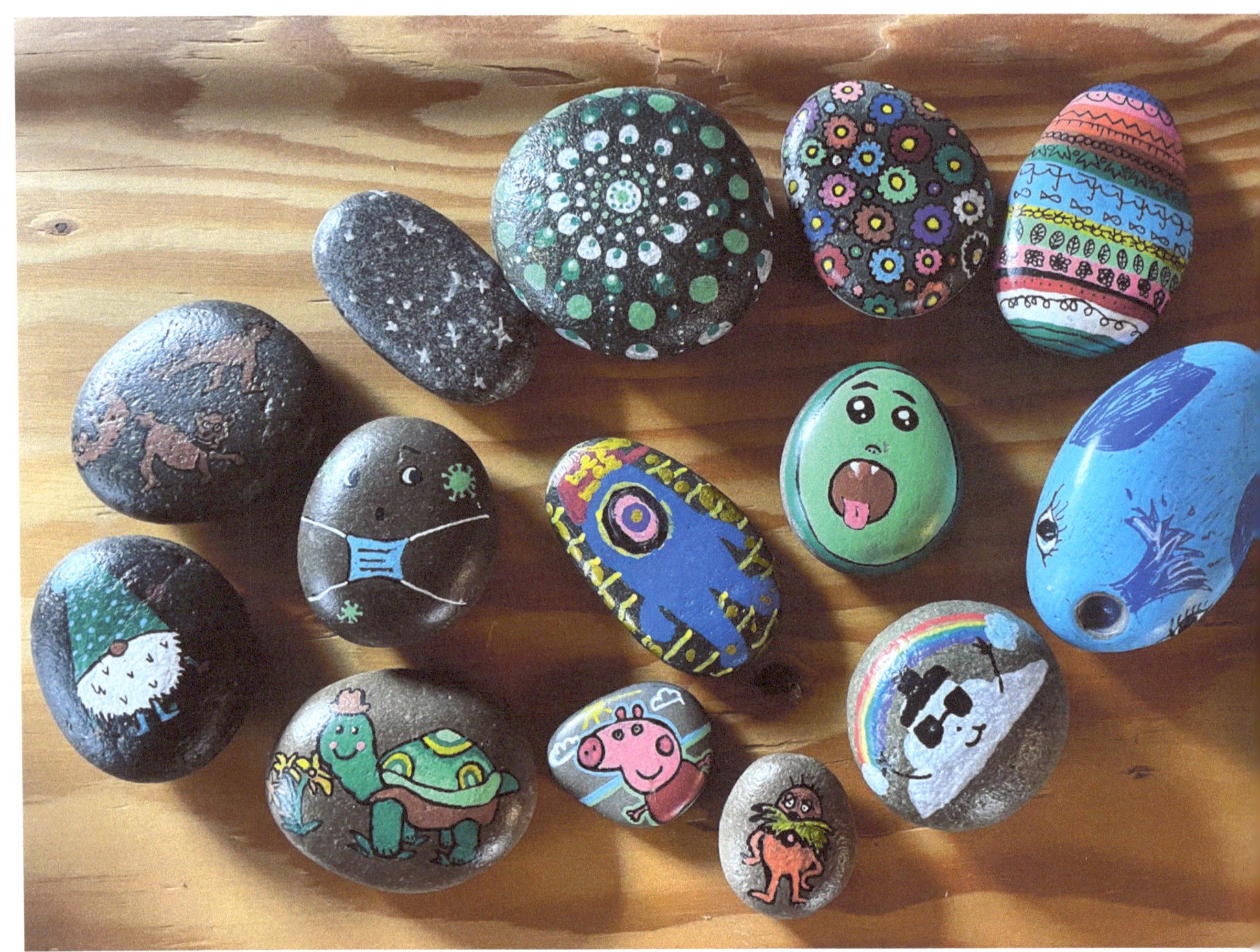

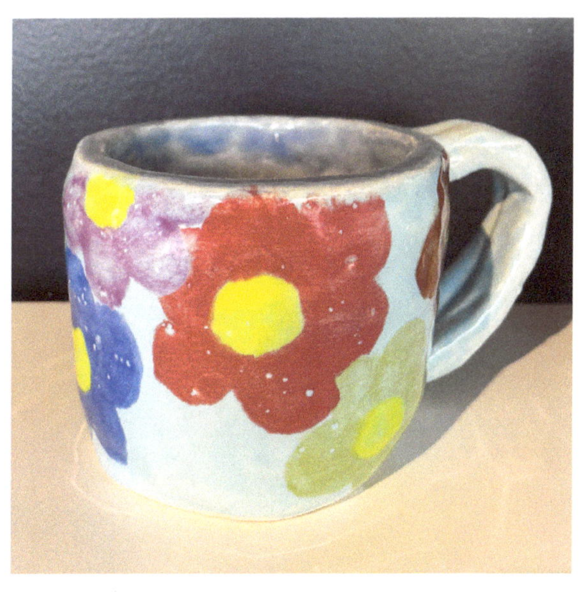
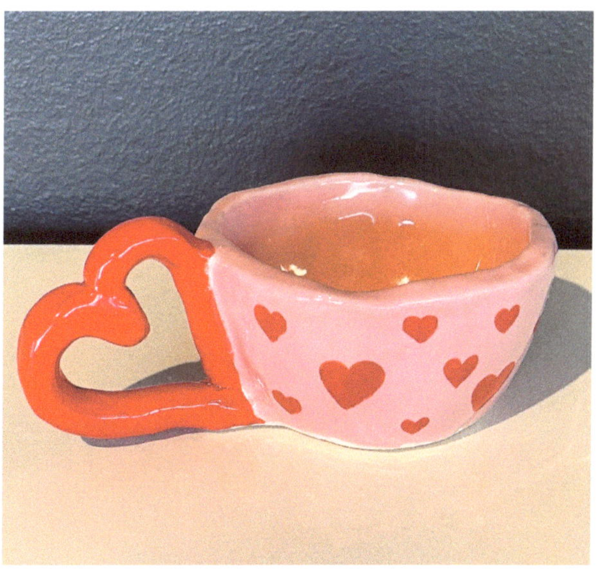
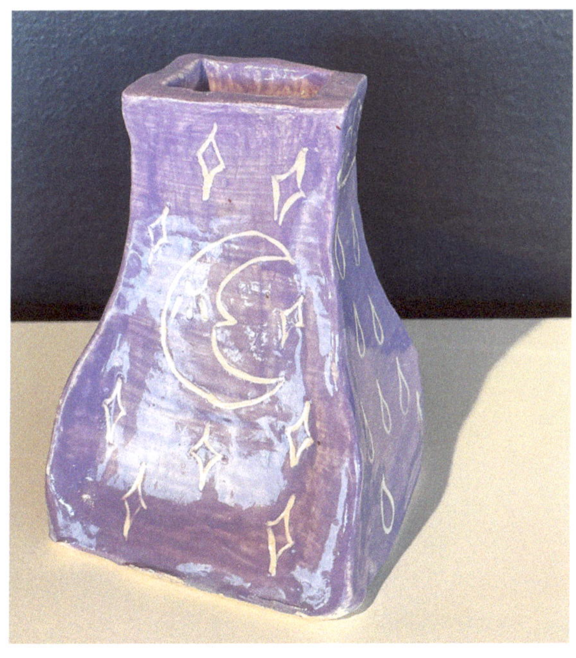
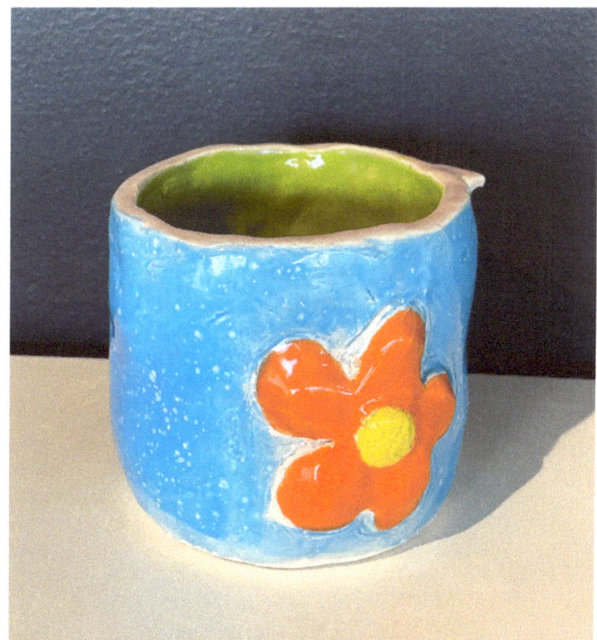

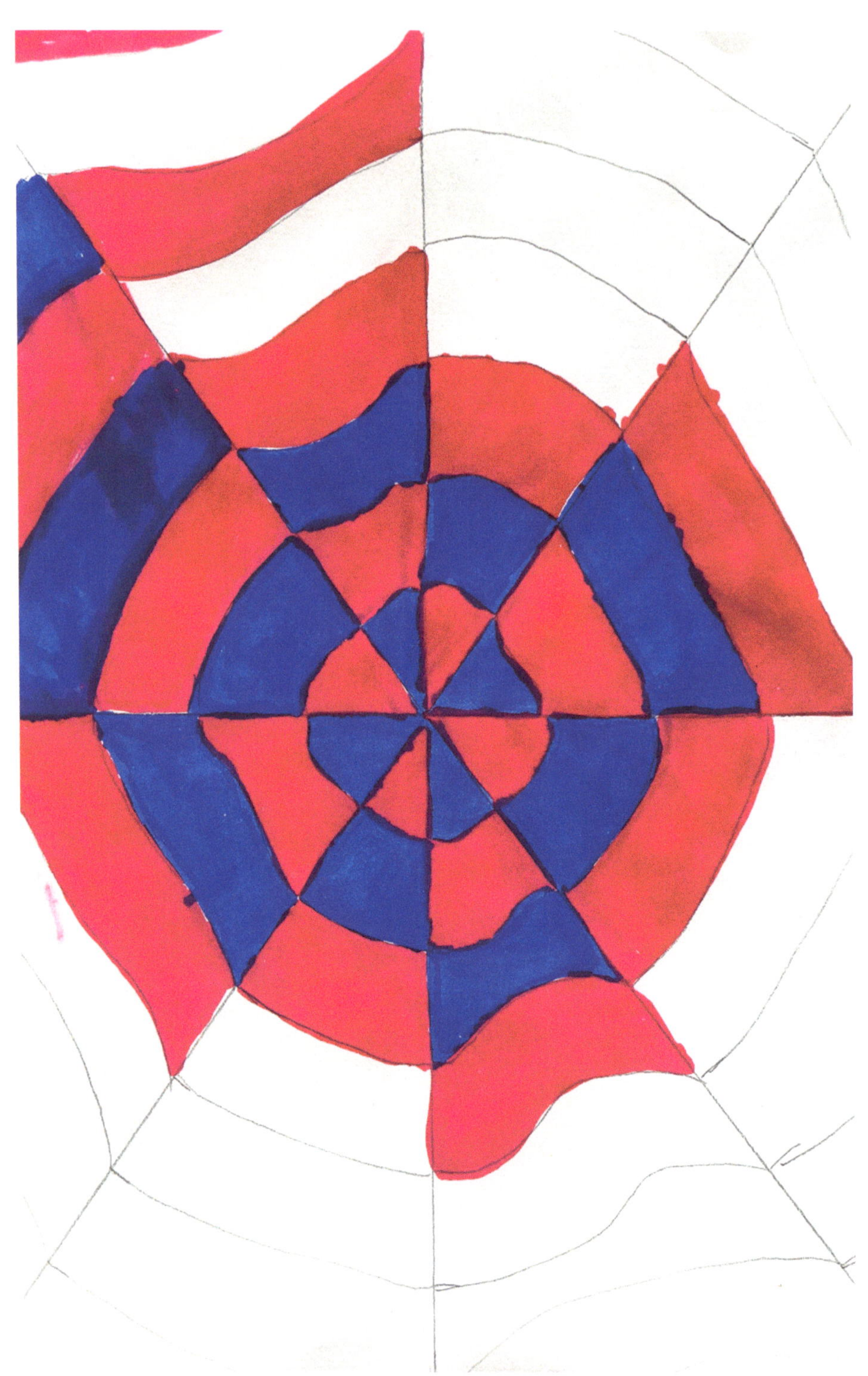

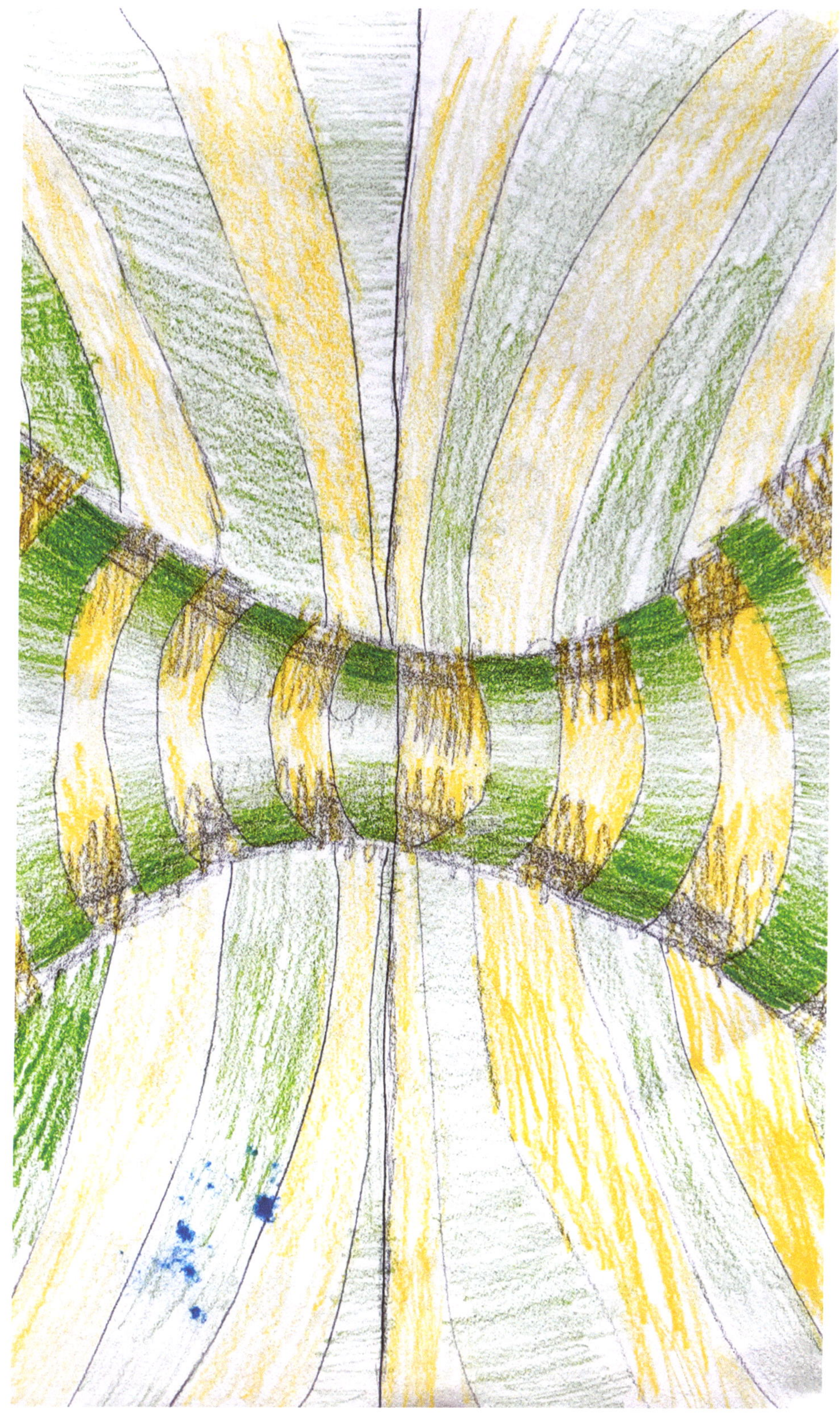

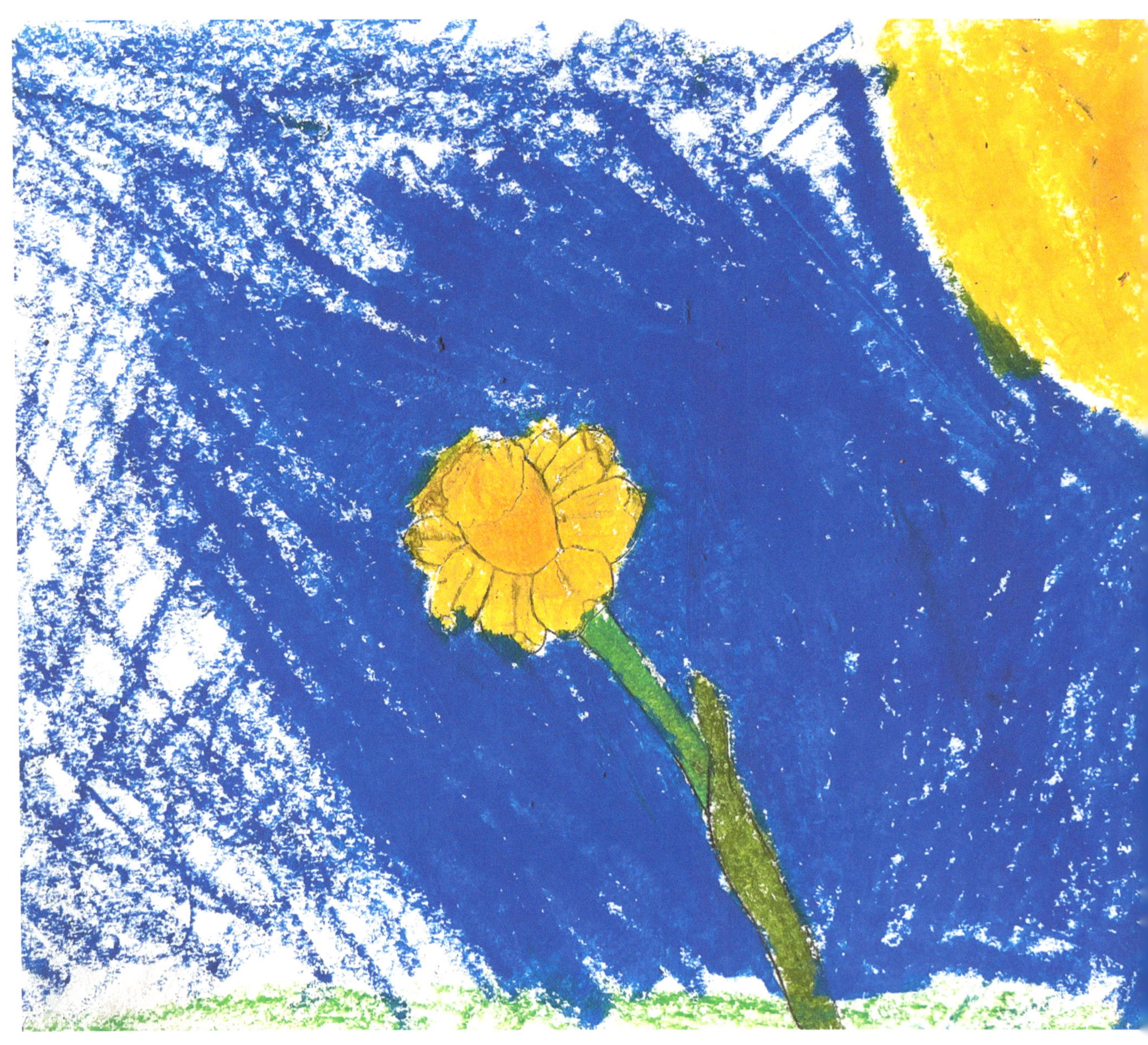

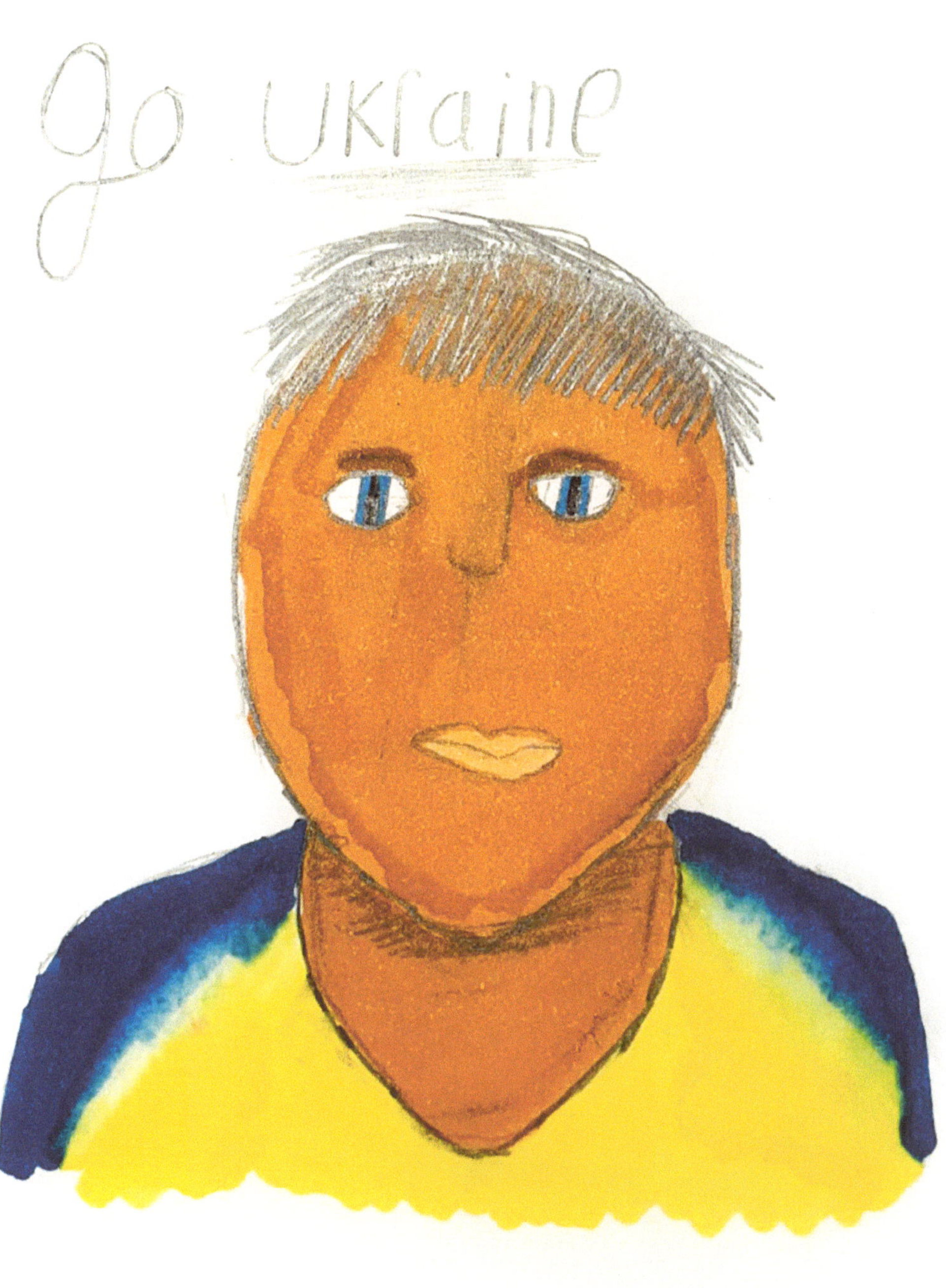
go ukraine

There was once an evil train station, it was as evil as it got. If you said it wasn't evil, you would probably get arrested. That is because it was really really evil. Todd was an elderly adolescent. He worked at the Evil Train Station HQ. That was where all of the evil conductors did their evil deeds. The actual train station was just the center where all of the other unrelated evil dudes met up and made an evil plan. The actual fun stuff happened elsewhere. Oh, and there was the Green Giblin, we won't talk about him now, but he will play a major role later (very important).

One day when the bears were hibernating and the dogs were barking, the evil dudes made an evil plan. Their goal was to betray the evil train station and become the evil lords 😈😭🥶💀 !!!!!!! They would first arrive at the evil train station and then have an evil breakfast that makes them barf out evil poison all over the evil train station and destroy their evil home once and for all!

Tony would be the one to start this evil plan. They started making the plan and a goal on how to execute it. Little did these evil dudes know, the Evil Train Station HQ was working on a plan to eliminate these evil traitors.

Oh, and it was another day in the evil train station with *extremely* powerful evil air conditioners. The evil dudes looked out the window as they worshiped their really evil and cool evil lord of evilness! Gerald

Geraldson. They giggled and gobbled at the nice turkey knocking at the door and then it got stabbed by an evil chicken behind it. They were quite the goofers and goobers.

They began to create their evil breakfast. That was when a young lemon knocked on their door. She wanted to spend her last moments as a lemon with some nice people. She told them about her curse, she was cursed to one day become an old lady, and no longer a lemon. They closed the door on her and got back to their evil plan. They added evil potions, and more stupid junk. The evil train station was talking about how they kidnapped Papyrus from Undertale and ate him. The evil train station employees were busy eating raw metal because they thought it tasted good. They were also blasting the A.C because the evil train station employees were each required to wear 80 pairs of thermal underwear.

The next day, the evil dudes ate their evil breakfast and started to barf up a bunch of poison. They all grew four eyes because of the radioactivity. Little did they know, the Evil Train Station HQ had made a love potion to throw on the evil dudes!

They threw the potion on the evil dudes and they all started hugging. It turns out it was just water but thinking it was a love potion they fell into peaceful harmony.

CLARA ROWE

Age 6, Long Island, NY

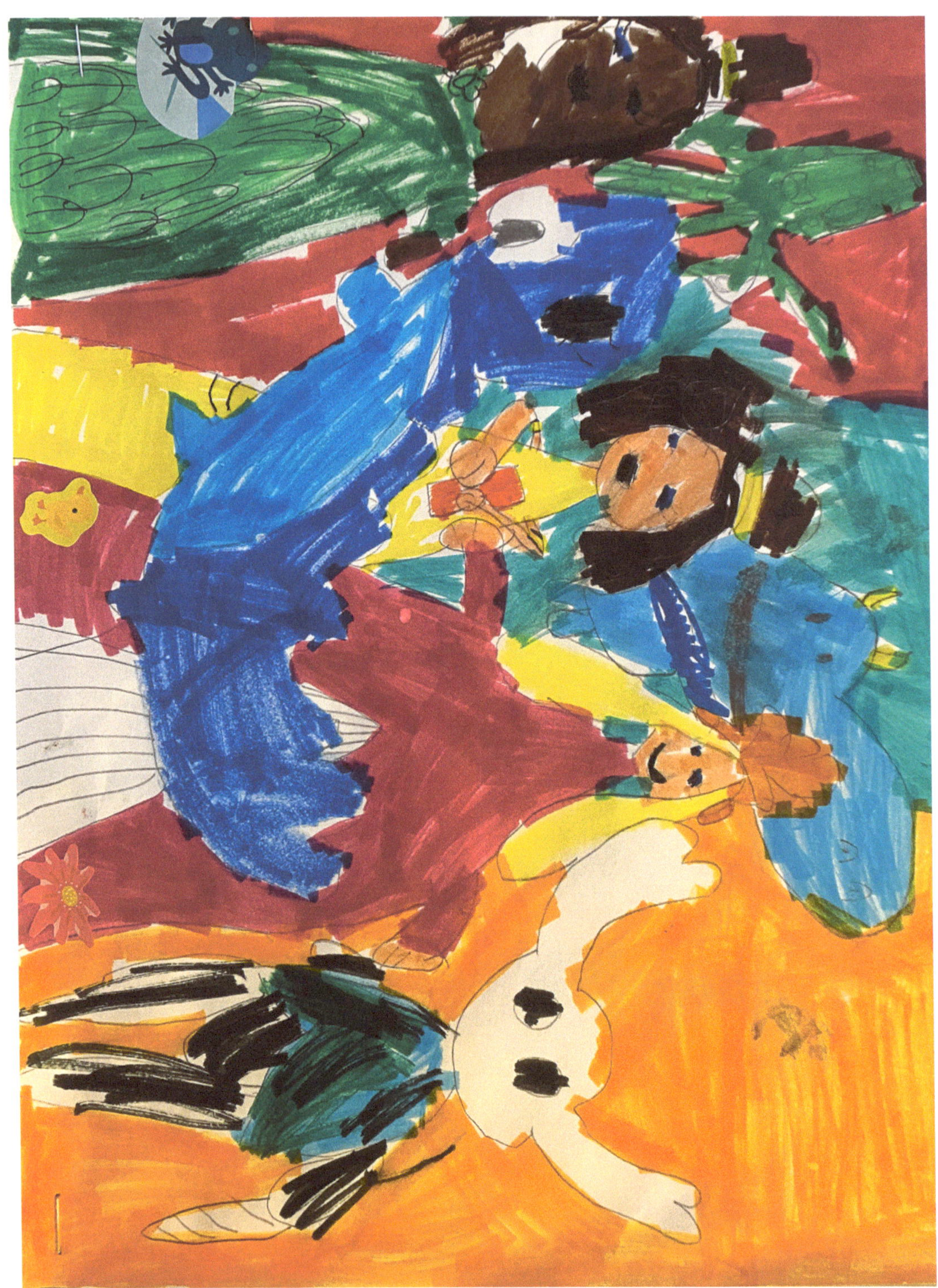

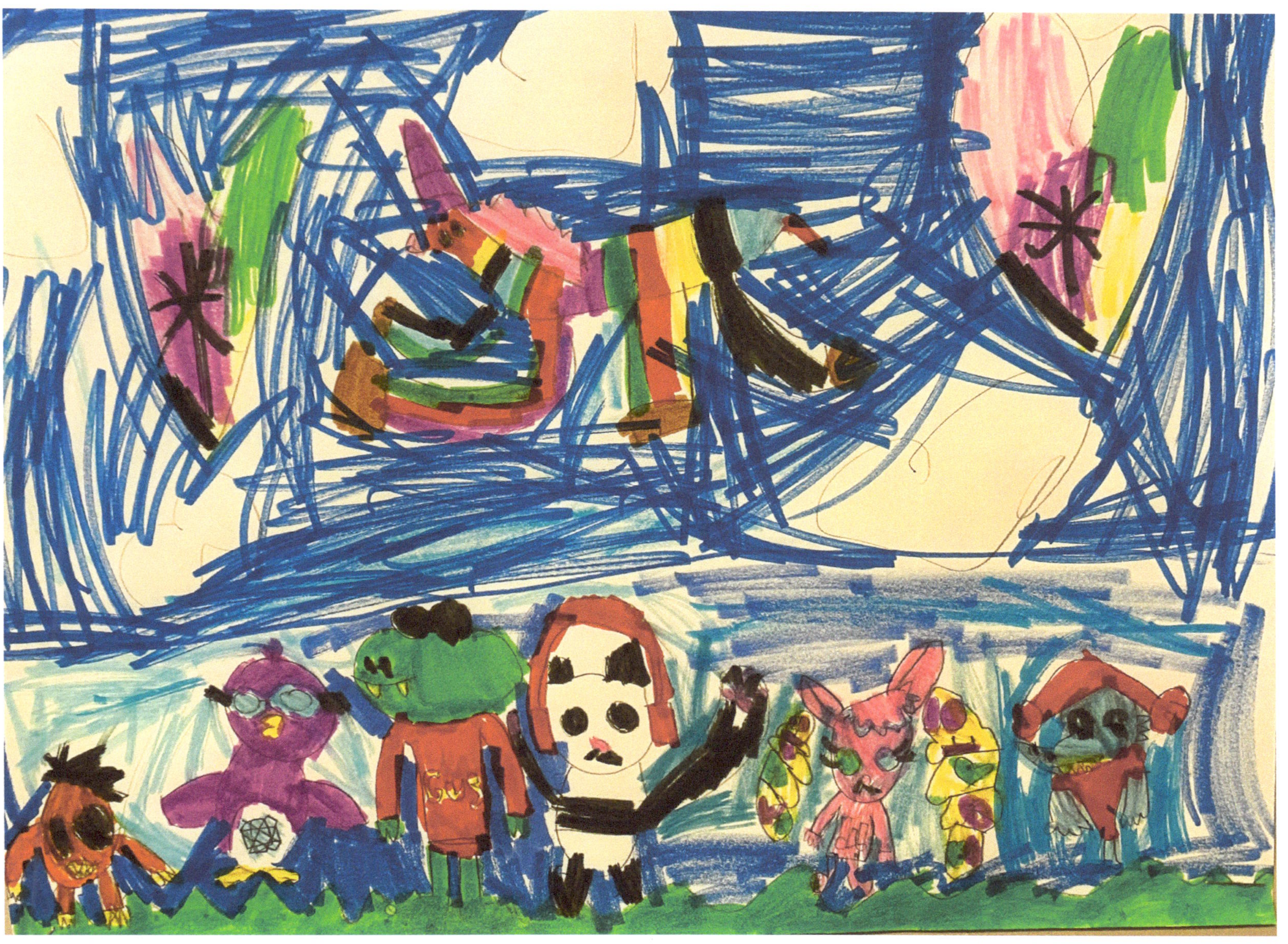

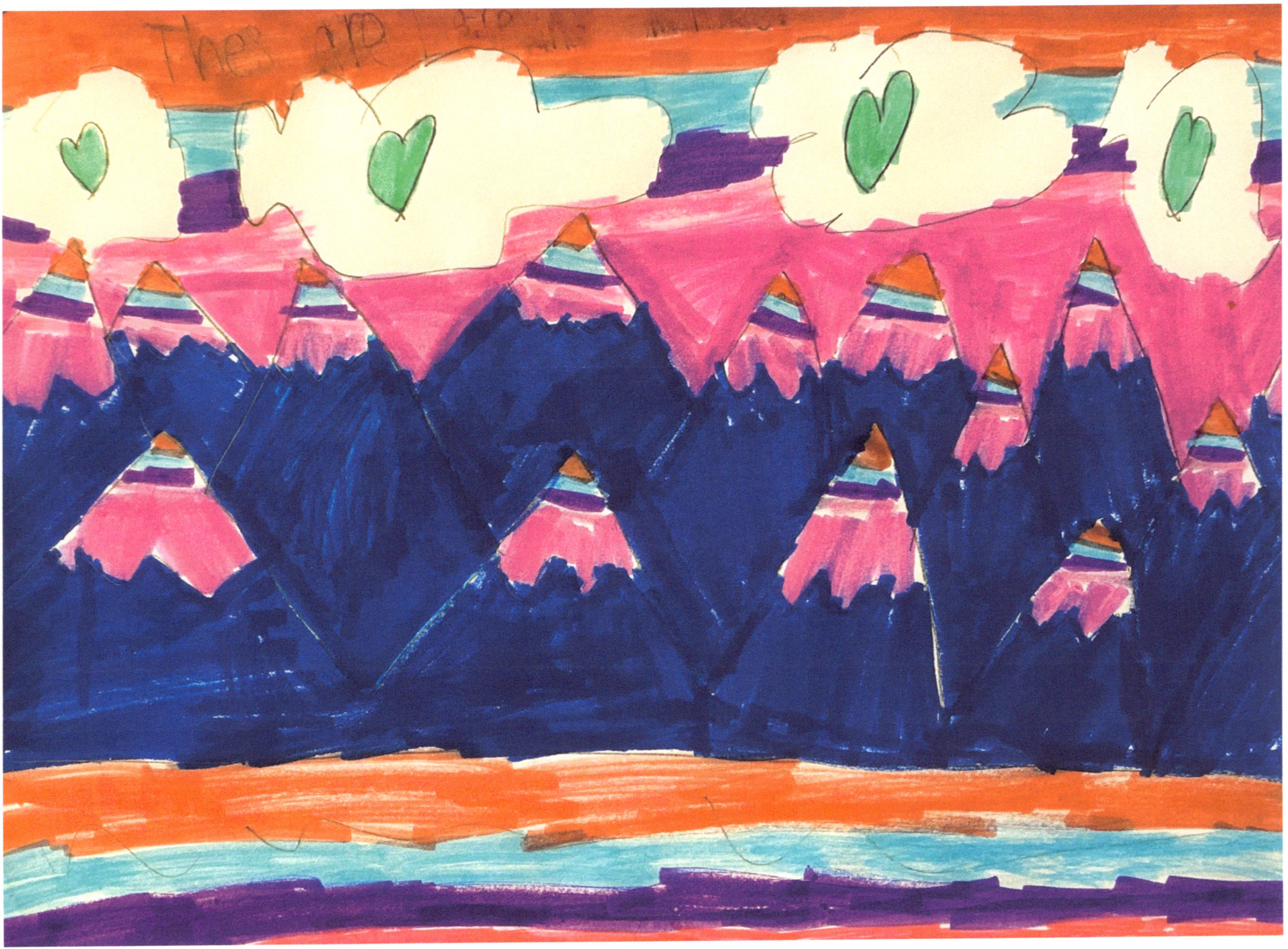
They are

ELIOT (ILYA) DORA

Age 5, London, UK

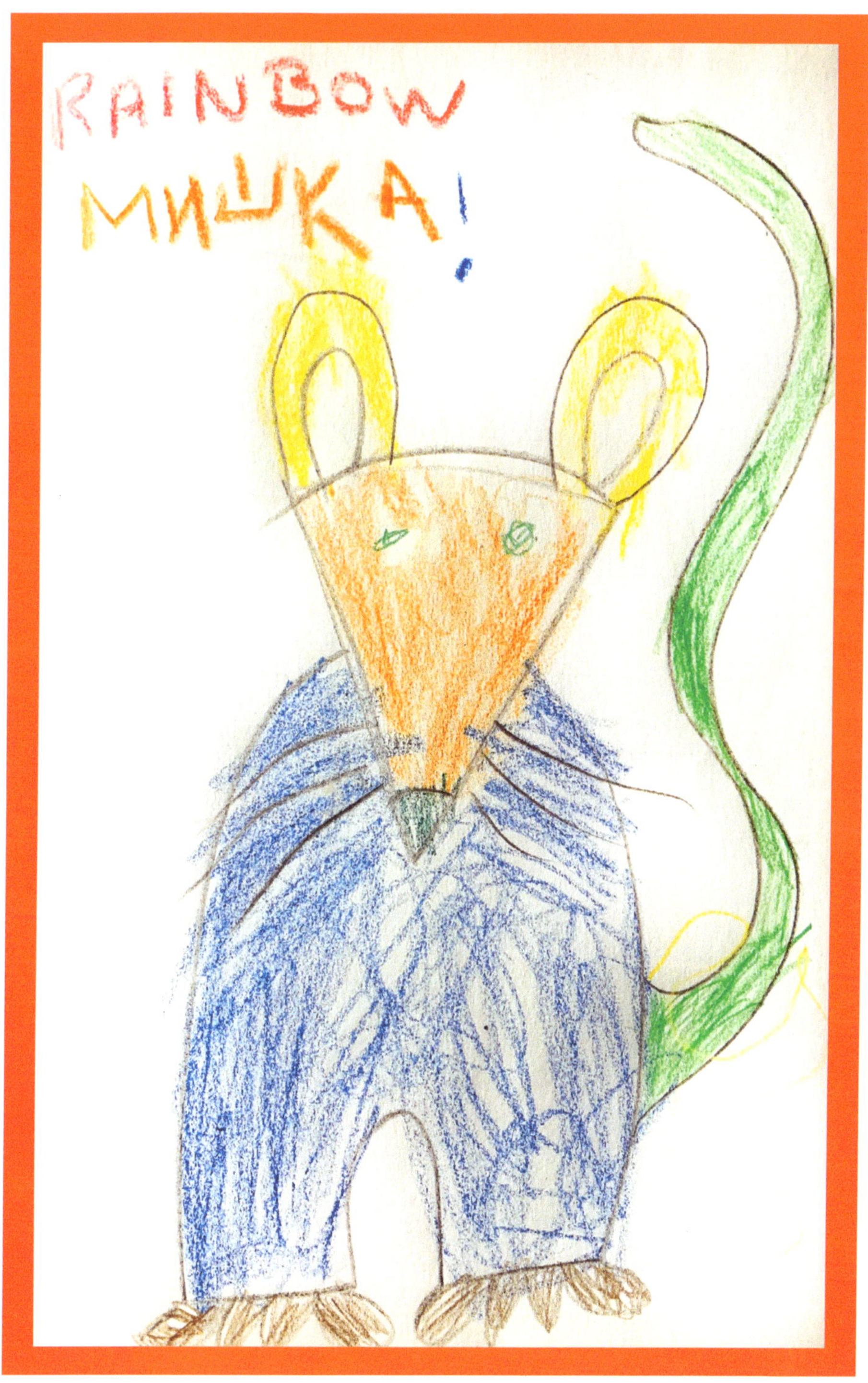

Elliot

PARKER GREENBERG

Age 3.5, Chicago, IL

A huge thank you to all of the participants who contributed their wonderful, creative work!

And many thanks to the adults who supported this project through submissions and donations for Razom for Ukraine!

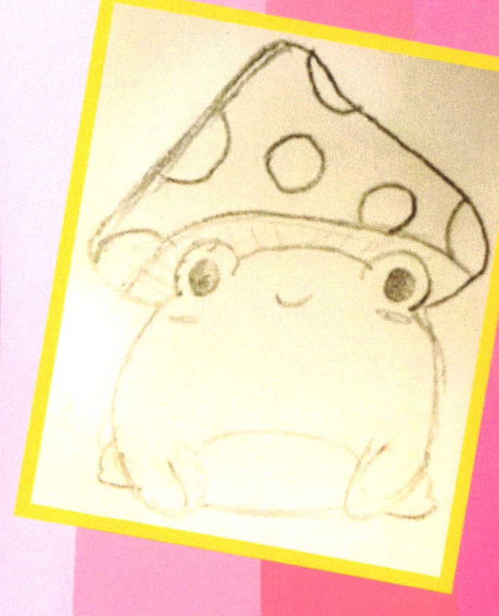

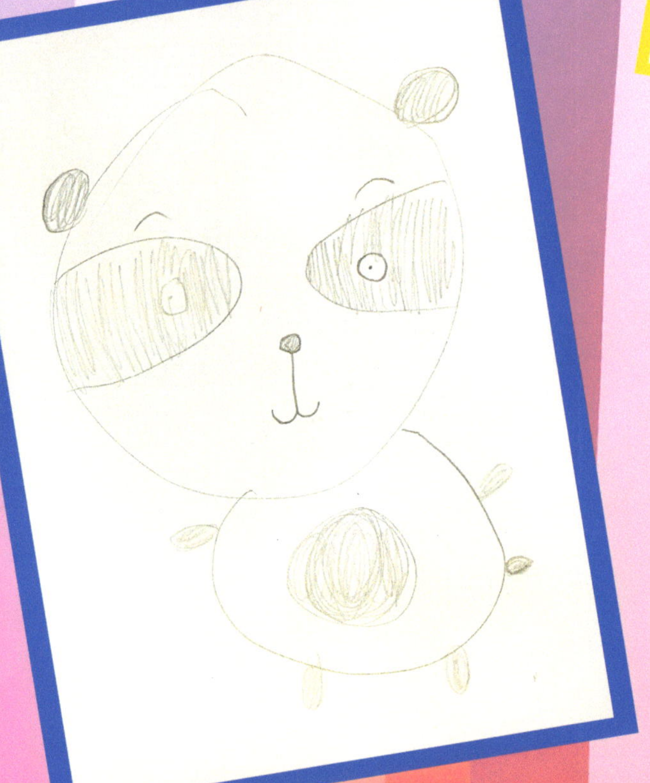

Panda and frog by my daughter, Maude Welker.

Нехай незабаром знову
прийде свобода і мир.

(Nekhay nezabarom znovu pryyde)

May freedom and peace
be yours again soon.

Ми з Україною

(My z Ukrayinoyu)

WE STAND WITH UKRAINE!

Printed in the USA
CPSIA information can be obtained
at www.ICGtesting.com
CBHW042338010824
12554CB00034BA/376